Taking Sides

Taking Sides
OPINIONS AND MEDITATIONS

...

Keith McWalter

Copyright © 2016 Keith McWalter
All rights reserved.
ISBN: 1535542756
ISBN-13: 9781535542753
Library of Congress Control Number: 2016913991
CreateSpace Independent Publishing Platform
North Charleston, South Carolina

For Courtney, again

Contents

Introduction ·ix

The Law and Lawyers
Legal Journalism and Gay Rights · 3
Right Result, Wrong Venue: Gay Marriage and the Supreme Court · · · 8
How to Negotiate Like a Crazy Person · 13
Taking Sides: Scalia and the Politicization of the Supreme Court· · · · · 16
The Iran Nuclear Deal: 5 Rules of Negotiation · · · · · · · · · · · · · · · · · · 21

Writers and Writing
So You (Still) Want To Be a Writer· 27
The Considerable Merit of the *New Yorker* · 33
Flying with Saint-Exupéry· 35
Life's Reward: A Remembrance of James Salter · · · · · · · · · · · · · · · · · 39
The State of the Novel: *Fates And Furies* · 44
Welcome to Writer's Hell · 50

Politics
The Snowden Muddle · 59
What is Terrorism? · 62
Why is "Liberal" a Dirty Word? · 65
"Lucifer in the Flesh": Is Ted Cruz the Antichrist? · · · · · · · · · · · · · · · 69
Lawmaking Is Not Binary · 72

Politics and the War of Values · 75
Easy Targets: The Fun and Futility of Anti-Trump Journalism · · · · · · 81

Society
Can We Talk About the Fatwagons? · 87
The Duty of Intervention · 90
The Future of The Internet· 93
Is Our Entertainment Moral? · 96
Illiberal Arts: Does College Have a Future? · · · · · · · · · · · · · · · · · 101
Orlando· 107
How to Prevent the Next Lone Wolf · 109

Meditations
Anniversary · 115
The Lesson of the Two Shoes · 117
The Parable of the Asian Ladybug · 119
11/22/63 · 121
Last Chance Lost: Remembering Joel· 125
Love, Loss, and Social Security· 133
Life in the Silos · 136
The Last Place · 140

About the Author · 145

Introduction

• • •

THE THIRTY-THREE PIECES IN THIS collection were written over a span of three years, up to the summer of 2016. All of them first appeared in the blog *Mortal Coil*, started eleven years ago on the premise that this relatively new form of online expression might be a useful outlet and archive for assorted short material that I felt compelled to write, but that might not otherwise see the light of day.

Writing is indeed a compulsion for some of us; we would write even if what we wrote were never read. But it helps to have an audience. When I was a young man starting out in New York City in the '70s, I would write long, academic essays on politics and society to my college friend Paul Dimitruk, who was living at the time in far-off San Diego. They were like term papers without the term, the kind of ruminative writing that I'd had to unlearn in law school, and Paul was the only person I knew who I thought might tolerate it. I wrote those essays on erasable paper on the portable Olivetti typewriter that I'd used in college for actual term papers and, since what would become the Internet was at the time unknown to anyone but the Defense Department and a handful of wonks at Stanford, folded them up in manila envelopes and mailed them off to him by way of physical mail (which we called, simply, "mail"). I don't recall that he responded with much more than puzzled silence, but I now see that this was an early and extremely cumbersome form of blogging.

Later, when I was in my forties and working too hard, on the long flights I regularly took between San Francisco and New York, I'd order a

Bloody Mary, pull out my yellow legal pad and take inventory of my life, with headings like "Problems" and "To Do." In the latter column I would invariably instruct myself to "Do more writing," knowing that I didn't have time for it. Now I do.

It still helps to have an audience, and the very existence of *Mortal Coil* provides at least the premise of one, just as an empty theater silently demands that something be staged there. Each new post may only be read by a hundred or a handful of people who may stumble across it in a Facebook link, but I try write it as though its destination were the *New York Times*, which, in another, less agented era, regularly received my essays "over the transom," as the quaint expression goes, and occasionally published them. (I've thought of changing the name of the blog to "The Transom.")

The personal essay, though ancient (one thinks of Montaigne scribbling away in 1580), is perhaps the least commercial form of writing, somewhere behind poetry in market potential. It relies entirely on the reader's transient resonance with the subject, and her acceptance of a certain conversational voice. As in a real life conversation, if you don't relate to that voice or that subject you quickly move on. So I hope the reader of this volume will feel free to browse, rather than dutifully read front-to-back.

The title of the collection is both descriptive and cautionary; only when no one can stop you, as when you put up a blog, or own a newspaper, can you give full vent to your unsolicited opinions; no one will pay you for them, unless you're an ex-President or George Soros. But then again, to receive nothing in exchange for views no one asked you for is not an unfair trade.

Many of the essays this book take the form of an op-ed piece, and several of them started as mental rejoinders to actual op-eds in the *Wall Street Journal*, perhaps my single greatest source of counter-inspiration. (My wife would look up from our breakfast table to find me staring off into space, the op-ed pages of the WSJ spread before me. "Blog?" she'd ask knowingly.) For other provocations, I'm indebted (and I mean this sincerely) to my friend Paul, a principled conservative, and his friends and family, who have kept me aware, sometimes painfully, that my own political predispositions are not universally shared, but also that rational conversation across great divides is still possible.

The pieces are grouped in very general categories, and within each are not in rigid chronological order (the date of original posting is noted after each), but rather are sequenced as their topics seemed to suggest. Some have been mildly tweaked; the occasional word choice improved, some titles revised to better reflect their subjects.

The three years in which they were written culminate in an election year, also one of the most tumultuous years of the decade, in which mass shootings, terrorism, racial unrest, and outrageous political spectacle became our daily fare. Hence the section on politics, in particular, may soon (one can hope) seem like ancient history, but will perhaps preserve some snapshots of what provoked and frightened us in this bizarre interlude in our national life.

Other subjects are, I hope, more enduring: the importance of mentors, both actual and literary; the ineradicable imprint of certain moments in personal or national history; the transporting joy of reading, the duty of writing, and finally, what James Salter, remembered here, called "the glory of certain moments in life," by which he meant unimportant moments, ahistorical moments, moments that might pass unspoken, but sacred nonetheless.

August 2016
Granville, Ohio

The Law and Lawyers
• • •

Legal Journalism and Gay Rights

• • •

As I write this, the Supreme Court's rulings on the Defense of Marriage Act (DOMA) and California's Proposition 8 have just been announced, and the airwaves and cables and Internet are full of truly awful reporting on these important cases. I welcome the outcomes in these cases both as just results and as good Supreme Court and Constitutional housekeeping, but I deplore the news media's inability to grasp nuance or resist sensational overstatement in matters of such national importance and interest.

Rachel Maddow has just declared that, as a result of the rulings, the issue of gay marriage "is now decided as a nation. The argument is won." Well, no. Love ya, Rach, and love your hair, but the idea that we've all coalesced into one harmonious, gay-embracing mass due to a couple of edicts of a bunch of jurists in Washington is just wishful thinking, as silly as the idea that Obama's victory last November showed Republicans the error of their political ways. No, and no.

Soon after the two decisions were released, some female desk-jockey on CNN whose producer thinks making her wear black-framed glasses makes her look intellectual announced that "gay marriage has been legalized in the United States." Uh, no. This is not just bad reporting on the part of a major news organ; it's incompetent and cruelly misleading reporting.

True, I'm a lawyer and care more than non-lawyers about getting legal nuance right. But this isn't that hard, folks, and we deserve more from the people who are paid big bucks to mediate reality for us.

The DOMA decision is relatively easy to grasp: the Court struck down a portion of a statute, passed by Congress and signed by then-President Bill Clinton, that restricted the word "marriage," as that word is used in any and all federal laws, to mean the legal union of a man and a woman. The result of DOMA was that couples of the same sex could not avail themselves of the option to file joint Federal tax returns, or to receive spousal Social Security benefits, or to benefit from the spousal exemption from the federal estate tax, to name just a few economically-significant results, in spite of the fact that those couples may have been legally married under the laws of various states that have, in fact, legalized gay marriage. It isn't that hard for even the most conservative of jurists, no matter what they might think about the morality or advisability of gay marriage, to conclude that this works an adverse discrimination on certain legally-married persons and not on others, in violation of the "equal protection" clause of the U.S. Constitution. That's what a bare majority of the Supreme Court, led by Justice Kennedy, concluded and ruled. End of DOMA.

But it didn't take long for otherwise reliable reporters to get even this wrong. Renee Montagne, the usually sober-sided co-anchor of NPR's "Morning Edition," was heard to blurt to a legal expert she was interviewing soon after the DOMA ruling was released, that "this means that states can pass gay marriage laws with impunity, right?" The legal expert kindly refrained from laughing at her and instead said, uh, no, this means that gay people already married under state law can benefit from federal laws that were previously unavailable to them. It has nothing whatever to do with what states may or may not legislate with respect to gay marriage.

With the relatively simple DOMA ruling quickly muddled, there was little hope that the procedurally complicated Prop 8 ruling would be rationally explained. What the media were hoping for, and were at least potentially competent to digest, was a broad ruling on the constitutionality of Prop 8, which prohibited gay marriage per se by installing in the California constitution specific language to that effect. The conclusion that this, like DOMA, was an unconstitutional form of discrimination could have come under the banner of the equal protection clause of the U.S. Constitution (which trumps state constitutions).

However, where the Court can avoid deciding a thorny constitutional issue because of some technical defect in the proceedings, it often does. That is what it chose to do in this case. Rather than broadly rule on the constitutionality of Prop 8, it simply said that the private citizens who had brought the appeal of the case to the Supreme Court lacked "standing" to bring the appeal. Hence a lower federal district court ruling that the language of Prop 8 was unconstitutional under the U.S. Constitution was left standing. The result is that, as of now, the Prop 8 anti-gay marriage language is stricken from the California constitution, and gay marriage is at least not illegal in California (same-sex marriages can resume there once a judicial stay that was put in place to allow time for the appeals is lifted).

But as soon as the word "standing" became important to the case, you knew the news folks would never get it right. They can be forgiven: law students spend much of their first year of law school learning about standing to bring suit and the jurisdiction (or lack thereof) of courts to hear suits. In the Prop 8 case, the people that one would have thought would defend the law – i.e., the officials of the State of California, whose constitution was being litigated – chose to sit this one out (because, being liberal Democrats, they thought Prop 8 was unjust and had no interest in defending it). Instead, its defenders were a bunch of private right-wing ideologues who had originally marshaled enough signatures to put Prop 8 on the ballot (it was a voter referendum, after all). It was these people that the Court concluded lacked "standing" to come before it to make arguments in defense of Prop 8 because, in effect, they had no dog in the hunt: they could not show how they, as private individuals, would be affected by the outcome of the case, other than to have their ideologies offended (which has never been recognized as a badge of "standing"). In effect there was no Supreme Court case, and in turn no Supreme Court ruling "on the merits." Hence, the ruling of the last court that did have jurisdiction because the parties before it had standing (the gay men who were aggrieved)

– the ruling of a single federal district court judge in California - stands as law until overturned on a new appeal, should one ever be brought.

This sequence of events has been interpreted by Ms. Maddow, among others, as a declaration that Proposition 8 is unconstitutional and that "the argument is won," when the Supreme Court's ruling says nothing of the sort. The ruling was a purely procedural one, and its result affects only California, whose constitution was at issue. Indeed, my guess is that, if the current conservative majority on the Court had decided the Prop 8 case on the merits, it would have found no ground in the U.S. Constitution for overturning a duly-conducted state voter referendum, especially given that they had just eliminated one of the equal protection arguments against Prop 8 by striking down DOMA. The decision to reject the case for lack of standing was itself a 5 to 4 vote, with the four dissenters making up a group of very strange bedfellows, including the ultra-conservative Justice Thomas, who undoubtedly wanted to decide the case on the merits in order to uphold Prop 8, and Obama appointee Justice Sotomayor, who undoubtedly wanted to decide the case to strike Prop 8 down.

The difference between the Court's deciding the Prop 8 case on the merits and punting it back to the lower court is huge: the former course would have addressed gay marriage bans at the level of the U.S. Constitution and thus affected all 50 states; the latter affects only California (since that single district court judge's opinion of the Constitution can be ignored by the rest of the country, whereas the opinion of the Supreme Court cannot).

Why should all this be so hard for major news outlets to get right, even in the first half-hour of reporting? We have known for well over a year when these cases would be decided, and all the scenarios (including the remand of the Prop 8 case for lack of standing) were well understood, at least by lawyers. How could legally accurate and easily understood descriptions of all the possible outcomes and their consequences not have been written up and loaded onto the teleprompters long ago? Where is Nina Totenberg when we need her?

One obvious answer: it's better TV (or radio) to be obtuse about it. Sensationalism sells, and accurately reporting the rules of civil procedure does not.

Still, all in all, a happy day for those of us who believe in human rights – if not for those of us who look to news media for help in understanding daily events.

June 2013

Right Result, Wrong Venue: Gay Marriage and the Supreme Court

• • •

THE RECENT SUPREME COURT DECISION in *Obergefell v. Hodges*, extending the right of same-sex couples to marry to all 50 states, represents a joyous, much-deserved victory for gay Americans and for all of us who have long wished for our gay friends and loved ones the same rights that straight people enjoy. As public policy, the ruling is just, sensible and, if anything, overdue. But as an undeniable instance of judicial activism, it joins a long line of cases where the personal beliefs of the justices mattered as much or more than the legal principles at play. Much as we might applaud this particular outcome (and I do), the judicial shoe may next time be on the other foot.

In a case like this, where the outcome is as I think it should be, I'm glad to have a majority of the Court ignore the fact that the Constitution is utterly silent on the subject of marriage and that, throughout the history of the republic, marriage law has been, with very limited exceptions, the exclusive province of the various States. I am happy to have the Court forget that the *Windsor* ruling of two summers ago, which struck down the federal Defense of Marriage Act, did so in part on the ground that state marriage law (allowing same-sex marriage in that case) should be respected, and that DOMA "depart[ed] from this history and tradition of reliance on state law to define marriage." Come to think of it, I would like a majority of the Court to completely ignore the Second Amendment too, as I regard an unrestricted right to bear arms as an antiquated and dangerous notion in the 21st century.

But if I like this ruling today, I'd better be prepared for the day when a majority led by, say, Justice Scalia, decides that the "right to privacy," on which Roe v. Wade is based, was just a dream we all had (as it, too, is nowhere mentioned in the Constitution), or that fictional legal entities such as corporations have the right of free speech (oops, that one already happened).

No matter how one regards the fact of homosexuality or the nature of marriage, even the most hard-nosed, Bible-thumping Federalist could concede that the spectacle of a couple legally married in one state but finding their union discredited by another was, in today's mobile society, an untenable absurdity that demanded correction. Last week's ruling, of course, went much further than that, concluding that the right to marry is one of the rights, protected by the Fourteenth Amendment, that are "so fundamental that the State must accord them its respect," and that a State's determination to legally recognize only marriages between a man and a woman violated that right.

This represents, in the view of an ever-increasing number of Americans, good policy; it represents equality, pure and sweet. But good policy does not always make good jurisprudence. The Court is in the unique position to impose the personal views of its members on the entire country, and that is precisely what the Constitution and the traditions of the Court forbid. That prohibition is the essence of judicial restraint.

The opinions of the four dissenting justices (Scalia, Thomas, Alito, and Chief Justice Roberts) all seize on this point: that five justices of the Supreme Court, with what the dissenters see as breathtaking hubris, presume to remove from the States and their citizens the right to determine how they wish to define marriage within their borders. Scalia is predictably scathing, denouncing his colleagues' majority opinion as "pretentious" and "incoherent," but also driving home with some humor the point that the Court is not – and should not act as – a representative legislature:

> "….the Federal Judiciary is hardly a cross-section of America. Take, for example, this Court, which consists of only nine men and women, all of them successful lawyers who studied at Harvard or Yale Law School. Four of the nine are natives of New York City. Eight of them grew up in east- and west-coast States. Only one hails from the vast expanse in-between. Not a single Southwesterner or even, to tell the truth, a genuine Westerner (California does not count). Not a single evangelical Christian (a group that comprises about one quarter of Americans), or even a Protestant of any denomination. The strikingly unrepresentative character of the body voting on today's social upheaval would be irrelevant if they were functioning as judges, answering the legal question whether the American people had ever ratified a constitutional provision that was understood to proscribe the traditional definition of marriage. But of course the Justices in today's majority are not voting on that basis; they say they are not. And to allow the policy question of same-sex marriage to be considered and resolved by a select, patrician, highly unrepresentative panel of nine is to violate a principle even more fundamental than no taxation without representation: no social transformation without representation."

Chief Justice Roberts makes the point more succinctly:

> "….this Court is not a legislature. Whether same-sex marriage is a good idea should be of no concern to us. Under the Constitution, judges have power to say what the law is, not what it should be."

Of course, this is a bit glib; the Court routinely says what the law should or should not be, as when, in *D.C. v. Heller*, it said that the law should not require guns to be under lock and key, or when, in *Citizens United*, it said that corporations should be able to spend whatever they want on political campaigns, Congressional legislation be damned. I don't like those rulings, but they sort of come with the judicial territory if I am to like the outcome of *Obergefell* (and I do).

Justice Roberts offered perhaps the slyest argument against the majority ruling:

> *"However heartened the proponents of same-sex marriage might be on this day, it is worth acknowledging what they have lost, and lost forever: the opportunity to win the true acceptance that comes from persuading their fellow citizens of the justice of their cause. They lose this just when the wind was at their backs."*

The "opportunity" to have to persuade others of our rights is one that most of us would gladly forego, thanks very much. Back in the Sixties, opponents of integration used to say that "you can't legislate morality." But you can; and immorality as well. We need look no further than Nazi Germany or the segregationist South for examples of the tyranny of the majority, where bad policy becomes law because the people will it, or just don't care.

Our ultimate – in some cases, only — protection against misguided majorities is the document that embodies our principles – the Constitution – and the body entrusted with interpreting it: the Supreme Court.

The Court could have taken a middle road: require the States, on the basis of the Full Faith and Credit clause of the Constitution, to recognize out-of-state gay marriages, but leave standing (at least for now) laws and state constitutions that ban the formation of gay marriages within their borders. Even that outcome would have produced absurd results, such as where Gay Couple A, legally married in California, moves to Ohio and settles down next to Gay Couple B, who cannot legally marry in-state nor, therefore, file joint state tax returns, while Couple A, legally married elsewhere, could do so. Marriage tourism would certainly have accelerated in such a patchwork legal landscape. But such a middle course might have had firmer Constitutional and precedential underpinnings than the rather convoluted (if poetic) interpretation of the Fourteenth Amendment that the majority relied upon, would have eventually required remedial legislative response, and would have made the liberal wing of the Court an example of judicial restraint to their conservative brethren.

The scorecard of judicial activism shows that when judges make law, everyone's ox eventually gets gored: *Brown v. Board of Education* on one hand, *Bush v. Gore* on the other. Sometimes you get a *Roe v. Wade* or an *Obergefell*, sometimes a *Citizens United* or a *Heller*. You win some, you lose some, in a game of Constitutional roulette largely determined by the philosophies of the sitting Justices at a particular point in time. This, and not any legislative agenda or foreign policy viewpoint, is why I will vote Democratic in the next Presidential election: I've become a Constitutional cynic, and the next President will likely nominate two or three new Supreme Court justices who will sit on the Court for decades, deciding cases that will shape our nation to a far greater degree than our dysfunctional Congress.

Would it have been better had the right of gay persons to marry been conferred by the will of the people at the state level, rather than by five jurists in Washington? Without question. Would it have taken too long? It had already taken too long, and might never have been achieved. Justice and equality were victors last week, as were we all, even those of us who can't yet abide the result.

But the fig leaf of Constitutional reasoning is barely visible in too many opinions of the current Court, and the naked ideology beneath all too apparent. We run the risk of becoming a nation of Constitutional cynics, content to let a panel of wise persons decide the gravest issues we face because we lack the collegiality, humanity or statecraft to address them in our legislatures.

We will be wise to remember: when the Supreme Court legislates, you win some and you lose some, and all too often, in Justice Roberts' words, "the Constitution ha[s] nothing to do with it."

July 2015

How to Negotiate Like a Crazy Person

(unsolicited advice to John Boehner and Barack Obama)

• • •

LIKE MOST AMERICANS, I'VE BEEN watching the current budget/debt ceiling crisis in Washington D.C. with a mixture of awe and incredulity: awe at the sheer recklessness of supposedly professional politicians in putting the nation's economy and fiscal reputation at risk, and incredulity at their seeming ignorance of the fundamentals of negotiation.

Most of these politicians are lawyers like me, and most of them must have had at least some experience in high-stakes negotiations, either as litigators trying to reach settlements, or (like me) as commercial lawyers trying to reach contractual agreements on behalf of their clients. Yet none of the principals in the current fiasco displays the slightest familiarity with the basic rules of effective negotiation that apply in the real world.

Hence, as a public service, I herewith offer a few dispute resolution techniques, drawn from the world of actual commercial negotiations, that might be of help in the current crisis:

1. **Don't Show Up.** Nothing befuddles your opponent, who may have gone to great effort and expense to meet with you, like simply failing to appear. Let him or her munch on those cookies in the conference room, wondering where you are and what on earth you

could be thinking, while you cool your heels back at your office, dreaming up your next snarky put-down of his or her position (see below). If he or she does eventually track you down on the phone, say glibly that there's no point in meeting to discuss things as your own position is so obviously correct, and besides you had a hair appointment. Likewise, make no effort at all to socialize with or otherwise get to know your opponent. It helps in this regard to assume an air of lofty remove, as though mere interpersonal relations have no meaning to a hard-working intellectual like you.

2. **Re-open points that are already settled**. Say you spent a couple of years closing your deal, the documents are signed, and there's even been a litigation over the enforceability of the agreement, resolved in your opponent's favor. Why should that stop you from trying to change everything you don't like about it? Insist on re-negotiating, and if your opponent balks, simply threaten not to pay what's been contractually agreed. When your opponent points out that it's a "done deal" (as we lawyers say), call him unreasonable (the absolute worst lawyer's insult).

3. **Offer nothing in exchange for what you want**. When you've exhausted your efforts to evade a meeting and do eventually sit down to talk turkey, be sure to insist that the other side give you 100% of what you want. (Every canny negotiator knows that if you start with a more moderate position, you might end up with some sort of compromise, God forbid.) When asked what you offer in return, act insulted and say that you're offering your opponent the opportunity to do what's right. Worth it just to see the look on his face.

4. **Exaggerate the consequences of compromise**. When pressed to explain your intransigence, say that any weakening of your position would mean the end of western civilization. Use those exact words.

5. **Insult your opponent**.   Your opponent may have law, logic, and precedent on his or her side, so be prepared to get personal. Attacks on his or her character, goodwill, upbringing, intelligence, patriotism, and/or taste will usually buy you time and may even

curry favor with your clients, who will assume you have something up your sleeve to save their bacon even if you're just ranting. And since everyone involved is a professional, these ad hominem attacks will be soon forgotten, won't they?

6. **Talk too much.** Once you have the floor, drone on about your position and its merits, and your opponent's position and its demerits, for as long as you possibly can – days, if possible. This can have the dual effect of forcing the other side to listen to your point of view over and over to the point of nausea and, when you resort to reciting Dr. Seuss, making them think you might in fact be quite crazy and capable of anything, which can only be to your advantage (see below).

7. **Employ the "madman" theory.** Made popular by Richard Nixon during the Vietnam War, this theory of negotiation holds that if your opponent believes you capable of anything, he or she will be more likely to give you what you want to avoid the consequences of your insanity. Hence if, for example, you appear willing to put your entire joint enterprise into bankruptcy merely to avoid coming to terms with the other side, the likelihood of their capitulating to your position increases exponentially. This technique can be extremely effective, but should be applied sparingly, since there is always the possibility that your clients also come to believe you are crazy, and fire you.

Some of these negotiating techniques may seem extreme, but rest assured that those of us who actually get deals done for a living have seen most of them in real life situations, and we can tell you how well they work, and how those who employ them are regarded.

Happy to help!

October 2013

Taking Sides: Scalia and the Politicization of the Supreme Court

• • •

THE RECENT DEATH OF JUSTICE Antonin Scalia closes the book on an enormously influential and in many ways exemplary legal career, and opens the door to a political knife fight that he probably would have found repugnant.

This blog has repeatedly focused on Scalia over the years, first in the context of the ruling for which he will probably be best remembered, *D.C. v. Heller*, which found in the Second Amendment an unqualified right of an individual to own and use firearms, and again last year when the Court legalized gay marriage in *Obergefell v. Hodges*, a decision from which Scalia dissented with characteristically withering disdain.

He was first and foremost a strict constructionist, as much an English professor as a lawyer, bringing an etymologist's eye to the interpretation of statutes and the Constitution. Ideologically, he was deeply conservative, a leaning that was for the most part well-served by his "originalist" judicial philosophy, which dictates that a jurist should be concerned only with what the original draftsmen of the Constitution (or of any statute being measured by it) meant when they committed its words to the page, and not with how those words should be interpreted in light of 21st Century reality, much less when subjected to the jurist's own personal predilections.

This is an important and credible viewpoint, even if you ultimately reject it (as I do) as a derogation of judicial responsibility, and Scalia was its principal champion for over four decades. It is the foundation of the concept of judicial restraint, which situates our court system, and the Supreme Court in particular, tightly within the framework of the other two branches of government, inhibiting judges from performing either the function of the legislature to write law, or of the executive branch to implement it. The courts, simply and purely, are to say what the law *is*, not what they might wish it to be.

The problem is that this is all very nice to say and almost tautological in practice. Judges in the real world deal with the same problem in thousands of cases every day: *how is a law (or a contract, or a constitution) to be applied to a fact pattern that no one who drafted it had foreseen?*

Scalia would say that the reason *Heller* was rightly decided and *Obergefell* is flat wrong is because the Constitution speaks of guns and the right to bear them but does not speak about marriage at all. And that's the end of it. Therefore, legislatures can deal with marriage more or less as they see fit, but can't touch guns.

But what the Constitution "speaks" of isn't quite the end of it. Contrary to what the NRA would have us believe, the Second Amendment doesn't actually say that an individual has the right to own any gun of any kind for any reason, period. The Amendment is qualified on one side with a preamble that is thoroughly bound to its time ("A well-regulated militia, being necessary to the security of a free State…") and on the other by a rather ambiguous statement of the right in question ("…the right to *bear arms*…"). (Note that I can "bear" a gun without owning it, and that therefore a good English speaker from Pluto might be justified in thinking that the right in question was the right to participate in a militia where I might be temporarily given a gun.) Historians and English scholars can and do differ reasonably on the question of what the draftsmen of that sentence meant by those words; their meaning isn't susceptible to empirical discovery, like the existence of Pluto, or to quasi-religious absolutism. Yet Scalia's stance was exactly that: there can be only one meaning, and I, Antonin Scalia, can discern it.

Scalia abhorred "judicial activism," epitomized in his view by the *Obergefell* decision, where judges take on the role of legislative bodies and right wrongs as they see them by interpreting source texts to meet the perceived needs of the moment. But as in the case of the Second Amendment, there is almost always a gap between what the Constitution says on its face and what Scalia and other originalists conclude that it is saying, and that gap can only be closed in the same way that the majority in *Obergefell* filled the undeniable gap between the Fourteenth Amendment and the outcome of marriage equality: by fashioning, out of less than perfect sources, what they *believe* to be a just result under the here-and-now facts and circumstances presented to them.

And so we are back to ideology and, unavoidably, back to politics. Scalia is dead (ding dong), and Obama will nominate his successor. It is altogether proper that he do this; it's his duty under the Constitution. Equally inevitable, but less proper, is the Republican pledge to "delay, delay, delay" (as Trump so eloquently put it) any consideration of that nominee until after a new president is installed in office next year (which, if that new president is also a Democrat, will mean that Republicans will have inflicted upon themselves, to no advantage, any number of possible 4-to-4 decisions that will effectively neuter the Supreme Court and affirm, by default, lower court opinions that they may not like at all).

But leave aside the fascinating range of political tactics and consequences that can be spun out of this; the deeper question is why we tolerate – even embrace – the spectacle of a bunch of politicians turning the highest court in the land into a stage for their ideological posturing? Why has the nomination of a justice to the Supreme Court become just one more occasion for taking sides?

A fascinating graph published in the *New York Times* after Scalia's death depicts how long it took each and every nominee to the Supreme Court since Washington to be confirmed or rejected by the Senate. For the first 150 years or so of our republic, this took but a few days at most, except when a Jew was nominated (Louis Brandeis, nominated by Wilson, took 125 days). Things begin to go haywire during the administration of Franklin Roosevelt, when he famously took it upon himself to pack the court with extra members in order to get the New Deal ratified. After that, confirmation periods steadily lengthen: Potter Stewart (nominated by Eisenhower) took 108 days; Abe Fortas (another Jew), nominated by Johnson, took 100 days before his nomination was withdrawn.

The politicization of the Court reached a kindling point in the case of Robert Bork, who was nominated by Reagan and whose confirmation hearings took 114 days before he was rejected. An ideological fist fight over Bork's nomination was perhaps inevitable, as he had been Nixon's Solicitor General during the Watergate scandal and had, at Nixon's behest, carried out the firing of independent counsel in an attempt to head off the unraveling of his administration. Bork, like Scalia (who was also nominated by Reagan), was a hard-core originalist who thought the "right to privacy" (on which *Roe v. Wade* was founded) was a fiction concocted by over-activist Supreme Court majorities. His nomination was fiercely and successfully contested by Ted Kennedy and virtually every civil rights and women's rights organization of the time.

Blame Roosevelt or Reagan, Nixon or Obama, but it's clear that Supreme Court nominees have come to be viewed not as jurists to be vetted for their legal acumen, experience, and impartiality, but as pawns in an ongoing ideological struggle through whom sitting presidents and senators can impose their values and politics for decades after they leave office. The Justices themselves are not blameless in this regard, as their self-imposed ban on making extra-judicial statements about issues of the day seems to have weakened in recent years, with Scalia himself leading the charge. The Court has been thoroughly and overtly politicized, and its opinions read less and less like legal analyses and more and more like position papers.

There is irony in the fact that conservative Republicans, most of whom adored Scalia and claim to share his disdainful views of judicial activism, have chosen to cast the pending nominating process as another pitched battle over ideology, since this implies not only that they view all judges as "activist," but that *they want them to be*. Scalia would have been the first to admit that he was an ideological conservative, but the last to consciously allow that to influence his opinions. To oppose a nomination to the Supreme Court in principle because one dislikes the politics of the President is to assert that judicial impartiality is a fantasy, and everybody knows it; all we are doing here, in effect, is hiring another lawyer to fight for our agenda.

I wish I could argue that this doesn't have to be this way, that we as voters could rise up and force our elected representatives to behave themselves in the matter of Supreme Court appointments, but I'd be blowing smoke. We have become a nation of Constitutional cynics, who believe not that the Supreme Court exists to discern and apply irreducible principles independent of politics, but rather that it is merely another, smaller legislature where we want our biases to be implemented.

I'm as bad as the next person in this regard; the primary reason I will vote Democratic in November is because I assume that the next president will nominate two or three new Supreme Court justices who will sit on the Court for a generation, deciding cases that will shape our nation to a far greater degree than our dysfunctional Congress. We've sown deep political partisanship in each of the other two branches of government, and we will reap what we've sown in the future decisions of our politicized Supreme Court. It will probably take a true crisis, Constitutional or otherwise, to shock us back into some semblance of respect for this once-revered branch of government.

February 2016

The Iran Nuclear Deal: 5 Rules of Negotiation

• • •

WHEN AMATEURS – BY WHICH I mean non-lawyers – are obliged to read an actual legal document, such as the recent draft agreement with Iran to limit and defer its nuclear aspirations, they are invariably horrified. So complicated! So dry! So many time periods! So much ado about dispute resolution! These same amateurs often feel free to pontificate about how a particular negotiation should have been conducted. Critics of the Iran deal – even such legal luminaries as Alan Dershowitz — have claimed that too many concessions were made, both in advance and at the table, and that the U.S. displayed a pervasive ignorance of what Dershowitz called "Negotiation 101."

This focus on the nitty-gritty process of negotiation caused me to reflect on what I'd learned in my own "Negotiation 101" – the practical education in deal-making that I received in the classroom of commercial financing transactions over much of my career. The experience taught me a few key principles that always seem to apply when people come together to attempt to reach a formal agreement about something over which they may profoundly disagree:

Rule 1: Making it personal is always a mistake.
Rarely do negotiators represent themselves; they almost always have a client. Effective negotiators never forget that their client's goals not only

come first, they are the *only* interests that matter. If personal ego can't be left at the door, it will inevitably complicate the discussions and may even derail them. It's a subtle form of malpractice. The accusation that Obama and Kerry were more concerned about Obama's "legacy" in their conduct of the negotiations than in reaching a better deal is about as damning a charge as one could make to a team of lawyers, regardless of what you think of them as diplomats.

Rule 2: You will not win every point.
People who get to the point in their careers where they are leading negotiations come with a liability: they are not used to losing. They come to expect that they are so persuasive or that their client's interests are so obviously compelling that they should win every point. But not only does this never happen, it shouldn't. A counterparty, no matter how weak, who hasn't been at the receiving end of compromise is going to be a disgruntled and unreliable party to your agreement, and if you believe you should win every point you are probably in the wrong business.

Rule 3: Unless you leave the room believing you could have done better, you haven't been in a negotiation.
You may have been at a cocktail party or the opening of a play, but not a negotiation. Many of the finest negotiators I met in my career agonized over the points they had to give up, the miscalculations they thought they might have made. This comes with the territory of being a zealous advocate of your client's interests, and is a product of the fact that agreement invariably requires compromise. Good negotiators always think they could have done better, and the hard part is that they can never know for sure.

Rule 4: Someone who wasn't there will always second-guess the result.
This someone may be your client, or a fellow lawyer who watched from the sidelines, or someone who merely reads about the results in the paper. Second-guessing is always much easier than the task of the negotiator, it always hurts, and it's always necessary not to let it get in the way of your knowledge of what really happened in that room, and of the reality of Rules 2 and 3.

Rule 5: Reality always supersedes the deal.
This is the diplomatic and commercial equivalent of the military rubric that no battle plan survives the first engagement. Even the most formal agreements have lives of their own, and the parties act their provisions out (or not) in the real world, not in a conference room or in the sub-clauses of a document. This is part of the reason for all those time periods and provisions for dispute resolution. How a transaction plays out in the real world always differs from the letter of the document that embodied it. Not sometimes – always. And how the parties react to that reality, how they behave when confronted with those differences, is far more critical to the success or failure of the transaction than the hard-fought clauses that gave it life.

July 2015

Writers and Writing

· · ·

So You (Still) Want To Be a Writer

• • •

REMEMBER TUPPERWARE PARTIES? THE IDEA was that stay-at-home spouses – then called housewives – who were bored out of their minds and wanted to make a little of their own money, would become neighborhood distributors of Tupperware, a collection of plastic food storage containers. In an early form of direct marketing with a dash of pyramid scheme, these women would invite their fellow housewives to elaborate parties thrown in their homes where Tupperware would be sold and new distributors would be recruited. Everyone got dressed up and had a good time, but no one made any real money except the Tupperware company, and eventually, once the kids were grown, the housewives put aside their fantasies of making money from the comfort of their homes and went out and got real jobs. Cut to the Women's Liberation Movement.

The Tupperware party may be a relic of the Fifties, but the phenomenon of a bunch of people - predominantly women - enthusiastically pursuing the chimera of a livelihood while talking mainly to one other and being exploited by entrenched commercial interests lingers on in various forms. One of the most galling and exploitative is the current market for, and in, aspiring but unknown writers.

In the heyday of the Tupperware party, the discovery and publishing of new writers (meaning "unknown" authors of fiction, non-fiction, and poetry) was the exclusive province of a few brick-and-mortar publishing houses and periodical organs – Simon & Schuster, the *New York Times*, *Newsweek*, *The New Yorker*, etc. – that acted as gatekeepers to the world of Getting Published. There was absolutely no appeal from their judgment, since they acted as the sole arbiters of quality and taste in writing, as groomers and educators of new writers, and as the only available channels of marketing and distribution for writers' output (other than a few literary magazines of modest distribution and mostly academic interest, publication in which was a synonym for being "unknown").

In this former world, the path to publication for the unknown author was long, chancy, but well-understood: you majored in English, took a job as a teacher or college professor and wrote on the side, maybe took an MFA in writing or became a local journalist, wrote some more, and eventually, if you had the courage and the encouragement, began to submit your stuff to the gatekeepers. Almost always, your stuff was rejected over and over again, but you kept writing and subscribed to *Writer's Digest* and kept submitting and maybe eventually realized (since you read *Writer's Digest*) that you needed an agent (of which there were many even in those days), and you submitted your stuff to an agent and maybe he or she submitted it to the gatekeepers on your behalf, and your stuff was still rejected over and over again. And eventually, in virtually all cases, you put aside your fantasies of Getting Published and went out and got a real job. Cut to retirement.

Today is different, but is it better for the unknown writer? (To be clear, I count myself as one of these, though my stuff has occasionally been published by some of the old gatekeepers.)

The publishing paradigm for the aspiring writer has changed in a number of obvious and important ways, starting with the phenomenon of e-publishing. E-publishing means that the gatekeepers no longer control all the gates. Amazon controls some of them (though it looks a lot like another gatekeeper, and we'll come back to that), and there are little plots in the outlying sectors of the publishing plantation (blogs, online magazines) where a sharecropping writer can actually see his or her stuff, if not in physical print, at least on a screen. The territory is now theoretically infinite, like the Web itself, and there is room there for self-publication in a myriad of public platforms, from YouTube to Tumbler to the commentary on your trip to Aruba in your Facebook timeline.

There are huge trade-offs to this change. Most glaring from the reader's perspective is the trade-off between volume and quality. Internet commerce is driven by two engines: our bottomless narcissism, and easy access to means of expressing it. The flood of new writing on the Web is torrential, but the sole arbiters of its quality are, in most cases, the individual authors themselves. There are no gatekeepers, no plantation owners, to keep out the riff-raff. When you can set up a blog page in five minutes, for free, every person on the planet with access to a computer is a potential memoirist. As a result, most of the writing published on or through the Web is, to put it charitably, junk, and still more of it will never be read by anyone but the author. The world of writers (like that of other artists) has been radically democratized by the Internet but also radically debased, like a wildly inflated currency.

From the unknown writer's perspective, the trade-off is between access to publication *per se*, which has become astonishingly easy, and actual recognition, which has arguably become much harder to achieve. Back in the '90's I could (and did) submit essays to the *New York Times* "over the transom" (a charming old phrase that you can Google if you need to) with the reasonable expectation that they would be read and, occasionally, accepted. Now the place is like a bunker, heavily fortified with diversionary Web-presences and black-hole editorial email inboxes against the tidal wave of writing that is directed its way daily from every corner of the World-Wide Web. The odds of your un-agented, unsolicited piece, no matter how marvelous, being plucked out of this morass are probably worse than winning the jackpot on a lottery ticket, and certainly worse than it was in those supposedly bleak pre-Internet days when your only weapons as a writer were your typewriter and some stamps.

Ok, so even if it's harder than ever to get published in the old-school way (i.e., by an edited print platform), what about self-publishing? Even in the Tupperware days, you could pay a "vanity press" to have whatever you wanted put on respectable-looking paper and sandwiched between real, physical covers. This (or the electronic version of it) has, without question, become much easier and cheaper with the advent of such Web-based services as Smashwords and Amazon's CreateSpace where, for a few hundred dollars, you can produce a professional-looking physical or e-book and have Amazon stand ready to sell it. (Whether any copies are ever sold is a different question; Amazon doesn't market unknowns except through its own portals, like its "Kindle Singles" e-publishing platform, which walks, talks, and rejects like one of the old gatekeepers.)

Nonetheless, for many writers for whom the only satisfactory measure of their work is the knowledgeable judgment of others (emphasis on "knowledgeable"), self-publishing is thin gruel, maybe one step above leaving the manuscript in the drawer. If I self-publish my book on Amazon but nobody but my Aunt Polly buys it, has it in any real sense been published? (If a tree falls in the forest, is there sound?)

For some, self-publishing can be viewed as an entrepreneurial venture, sort of like selling pies to your neighbors in the hopes of someday opening a bakery (or like a Tupperware party). There is the tantalizing example of Hugh Howey, whose self-published dystopian novel "Wool" was eventually purchased by Simon & Schuster for a six-figure sum after years of author-driven promotion on the Web. (In a triumphant flourish, he sold S&S only the print rights and Howey retained the online distribution rights.) Exploiting such rare success stories – and the writers who have heard them — is the business of a whole world of seminars, conferences, webcasts, and online courses aimed at the unknown author who still believes that Getting Published by one of the gatekeepers is the only real game in town.

The exploitation of aspiring writers is in part the consequence of another aspect of the new publishing paradigm: that the gatekeepers, having been acquired by conglomerates, undercut by e-publishing and forced to minimize costs, have abdicated many of their former author-grooming, editing, and marketing functions, pushing them down onto the writer. Publishers these days expect the author to present her work as a finished, pre-marketed, high-yield product, not as some nascent work-in-progress that would cost them a lot of editorial time and advertising money and still mean a roll of the dice. Hence, many of the webinars offered (for a fee) by, say, *Writer's Digest*, instruct would-be authors not in how to improve their craft, but in how to create an online platform, build a personal following, hire a "book doctor," devise a marketing plan, and otherwise do the work that, in a prior epoch, had been the job of the publisher. There is a major industry, far larger and more lucrative than the Tupperware of old, built on convincing would-be writers that they need these skills and services, having nothing to do with the tedious terror of actual writing. This may not be progress.

Is today's world of publishing better for the would-be writer than the pre-Web world of the literary gatekeepers? I think not. You still have to write well, and you still have to have something worthwhile and interesting to say. Beyond that, today's confluence of too many liberal arts majors with too many computers has resulted in too many people who think they are writers – or could be – and print publishers have simply stopped looking for them. The merely possible begins to crowd out the good: even as the writer's self-help industry dispenses false encouragement, real-world publishers erect ever stronger filters against the rising tide of submissions.

How is the individual writer to respond to all this? To write at all is an act of ego: we believe our thoughts are interesting, entertaining, or informative enough that they should be committed to the page. It's a short step from there to the belief that others would love to read what we've written, or would even pay to do so. In vastly more cases than not, this belief is simply misplaced. This doesn't mean we should stop writing (a real writer probably couldn't even if he or she wanted to), but it does mean, first, that we should be tougher self-editors.

More importantly, we writers, even those few who have been published, need to learn to better content ourselves with the inherent pleasure of writing and stop distracting ourselves and lining others' pockets in our Sisyphean efforts to get the world to acknowledge it. We need to tamp down our narcissism and recognize the universal cultural urge toward fame for the waste of time that it is. If Getting Published is our only litmus test of whether we're good writers, we're probably not, because we're writing for some imagined audience rather than ourselves. This is not to say that if we write for ourselves and write well, such authentically good writing will win out, because it probably won't; the likelihood that it will has diminished, not increased, in the new world of publishing. We nonetheless need to write for ourselves, for the sheer love of the right words in the right order on the page, and perhaps for those relatively few others who might care to read us, even if they're only a handful of friends and family. We might never (or never again) be published in the old-fashioned way, and that's perfectly alright. It's time to go home from the Tupperware party.

January 2014

The Considerable Merit of the *New Yorker*

• • •

I'VE RECENTLY BEEN CATCHING UP on some reading and was completely gobsmacked (is this really a word? If it isn't, it should be) by a recent issue of the *New Yorker*, specifically the Feb. 17-24, 2014 edition. If you care about good writing on almost any subject, and better still if you care about lot of good writing on a variety of subjects, get hold of it. In this one magazine, thinner than most Eddie Bauer catalogues, were (i) a fascinating, balanced study of Attorney General Eric Holder by Jeffery Toobin; (ii) a poignant, funny, devastating, utterly lucid piece about being 93 years old by the redoubtable Roger Angell; (iii) an entertaining profile of Neil deGrasse Tyson, director of the American Museum of Natural History and star of the new "Cosmos" series on Fox; (iv) a challenging and remarkably erudite philosophical rumination by Adam Gopnik (whom I foolishly think of as that guy who writes a lot about living in Paris) on the nature of religious faith in an atheistic age; (v) a cruel but seemingly fair review of the movie "The Monuments Men," by David Denby; and, just for good measure (vi) a long, touching remembrance of Philip Seymour Hoffman, viewed entirely through the prism of his many movie roles, by Anthony Lane (no matter how foolishly one dies, one could do worse than to have such informed attention directed so keenly at what you'd spent most of your short life doing).

And that's just the stuff I *read*! There was also a piece on Turkish TV (hmm?), a short story by some Scandinavian author that I couldn't bear to read (but then I avoid fiction in the *New Yorker* as an almost religious matter, perhaps out of sheer unadulterated envy, or a long Ann Beatty hangover), some random short reviews of books whose titles told me unequivocally that I had no interest in them, and the usual comprehensive survey of stuff going on in Gotham. I only skimmed the piece on the "Financial Page" about the death of branding, though I suspect it was insightful too. And the cartoons were having a good week. Not a bad outing for one of the aging granddaddies of print media in its post-Tina Brown epoch. As John Leonard, patron saint of the personal essay, once wrote, "Some excellence came to our house the other day." And so it did to ours, delivered by our scary postman.

Ok, it's the *New Yorker* – it's *supposed* to be good. At its $7.99 cover price (which no one ever pays except some zeitgeist-starved desperado at a newsstand - and why not an even eight bucks, by the way?), it's not cheap, but I defy you to find so much worthwhile reading in one spot anywhere else. I'm sure they save all the good bits for this, their leap-month anniversary issue, but my God, what an amazing slush pile. Gobsmacked, that's me.

I once had a humor piece rejected by the *New Yorker* "despite its considerable merit," to quote the email that seemed to have been composed by an actual human. It was one of the proudest moments of my writing life. "Despite His Considerable Merit" would work well on my tombstone, I think.

March 2014

Flying with Saint-Exupéry

• • •

I RARELY AM MOVED TO tears by something I read. Our emotions are constantly tugged this way and that by the sea of media in which we live, and most of us have learned to swim against those currents, for they rarely take us anywhere meaningful.

But I just finished a chapter in *Wind, Sand and Stars*, the masterful memoir by the aviator-philosopher-poet Antoine de Saint-Exupéry, and with the final sentence, as I'm sure he intended when he set it down almost 80 years ago, he got me, all unawares, and I sat blubbering into my Kindle.

I've always loved flying as a passenger (once actually aloft and free of the multiform torments of airports), and have always regretted that I never learned to fly, imagining, as I imagine many of us do, that I would have had an instinct and aptitude for it (I love scuba, for instance, another application of technology to navigate an alien medium that requires calm and touch). By way of consolation, I read a great deal about flying, not so much about the technology of flight (which I understand better than most non-pilots, having spent much of my career financing commercial aircraft, visiting airline headquarters and aircraft manufacturers, and rubbing elbows with those whose business it is to vault large numbers of people through the heavens on a daily basis), as about what it is to be in command of a flying machine.

I came to Saint-Exupéry by way of other, later, pilot-authors whom I admire and who refer and defer to him in their writing: James Salter, William Langewiesche, Beryl Markham. From them and their rare ilk, I learned that Saint-Exupéry had paved the way in establishing the experience of flying as a legitimate subject of serious, non-technical literature. I finally got around to reading him rather than just reading about him.

Saint-Exupéry is best known in America as the author and illustrator of *The Little Prince*, supposedly a children's book, but full of the kind of philosophical rumination that permeates all his writing. In his homeland France he was and is an icon, revered as only the French revere their great artists. There is really no comparable figure in American culture — Hemingway, perhaps, but without the bluster and the dissolute end. Lindbergh, perhaps, but without the self-promotion and the fascism. Amelia Earhart (with whom he shared a pilot's fate), perhaps, but with the voice of a poet.

First if not foremost, he was a commercial and military aircraft pilot in the 1920s and '30s, when aviation as we know it today was just beginning to take shape, when aircraft made of metal were a new thing, and when meteorology and map-making were as much art as science. In these conditions he routinely piloted mail carriers and military craft across some of the most forbidding and then-uncharted reaches of the earth: northern Africa and southernmost South America. He crashed a lot, and seems to have viewed these events, for the most part, as minor interruptions in his duties. This is what the French mean by *insouciance*. His end was a natural coda to the narrative of his life: he disappeared in the midst of a reconnaissance mission over the Mediterranean in 1944.

Wind, Sand and Stars is a collection Saint-Exupéry's essays describing not only his adventures and mishaps as a pilot, but also flying itself: what it is like to pilot a plane in good conditions and bad across parts of the earth few men had laid eyes on, let alone flown over, and the emotions that attend the act of flying and the harrowing risks it sometimes entails. He of course wrote in French, so the prose in the edition I'm reading exhibits the affectations not only of period but of translation. Yet his language is startling, by turns gripping and lyrical, sometimes both at once:

> *When the night is very fine and you are at the stick of your ship, you half forget yourself and bit by bit the plane begins to tilt to the left. Pretty soon, while you still imagine yourself in plumb, you see the lights of a village under your right wing. There are no villages in the desert.... You smile at the way your mind has wandered and bring the ship back to plumb again. The village slips into place. You have hooked that particular constellation back in the panoply out of which it has fallen. Village? Yes, village of stars.*

Elsewhere he writes:

> *Pilot, mechanic, and radio operator are shut up in what might be a laboratory. They are obedient to the play of dial-hands, not to the unrolling of the landscape. Out of doors the mountains are immersed in tenebrous darkness; but they are no longer mountains, they are invisible powers whose approach must be computed....*
>
> *So the crew fly on with no thought that they are in motion. Like night over the sea, they are very far from the earth, from towns, from trees. The motors fill the lighted chamber with a quiver that changes its substance. The clock ticks on. The dials, the radio lamps, the various hands and needles go through their invisible alchemy. From second to second these mysterious stirrings, a few muffled words, a concentrated terseness, contribute to the end result. And when the hour is at hand the pilot may glue his forehead to the window with perfect assurance. Out of oblivion the gold has been smelted: there it gleams in the lights of the airport.*

In another piece he muses at length about the tragic folly of the Spanish Civil War, which he observed firsthand, and the folly of war in general. He was clearly in love with the austere people and inhospitable terrain of North Africa, and devotes long, insightful essays to their characteristics and travails, including a remarkably touching portrait of a black tribesman from Marrakech enslaved in Morocco whose eventual freedom was purchased by Saint-Exupéry and his fellow pilots, but who still had a different kind of freedom to find in himself.

And finally, he offers one of the most powerful and succinct survival stories that one is likely to read in his description of a terrifying crash in Egypt that left him and his navigator lost, on foot, in the middle of the desert without food or water and no way to communicate with the outside world except to burn their plane. It is at the end of this chapter that I burst into tears, the final sentence bringing into perfect, sudden focus all the relief and joy that the gritty narrative preceding it had rendered so thoroughly improbable. It seems to me that all subsequent literary depictions of survival in mountains, deserts and seas that I've read owe something to the harrowing realism that Saint-Exupéry establishes in these pages.

But he is above all a humanist, and a student and explicator of humankind. This is nowhere better captured than in the passage in which he describes (no spoiler here) the solitary Bedouin who saved him and his companion from the Egyptian desert:

> *You, Bedouin of Libya who saved our lives, though you will dwell forever in my memory yet I shall never be able to recapture your features. You are Humanity and your face comes into my mind simply as man incarnate. You, our beloved fellowman, did not know who we might be, and yet you recognized us without fail. And I, in my turn, shall recognize you in the faces of all mankind. You came towards me in an aureole of charity and magnanimity bearing the gift of water. All my friends and all my enemies marched towards me in your person. It did not seem to me that you were rescuing me: rather did it seem that you were forgiving me. And I felt I had no enemy left in all the world.*

Would that we earthbound writers were capable of such flight as this.

March 2015

Life's Reward:
A Remembrance of James Salter

• • •

It is not a life we are living. It is life's reward, beautiful because it seems eternal and because we know quite well it is not.

- JAMES SALTER, *IMMORTAL DAYS*

A LITERARY HERO OF MINE, James Salter, surely one of the most underappreciated writers of the last century, died last week at the age of 90. His passing, after a long and remarkably multifaceted life, is both a personal loss and the closing of a chapter of American literature.

Favorite authors hold a special and somewhat peculiar place in our lives — they're like celebrities who have befriended us, correspondents we've never met but whose inner lives we think we know, distant but admired relatives we can't visit often enough. Their books have been companions at turning points in our lives, or the books themselves pointed us in directions we might never have gone but for our having happened upon them. We are jealous of them, believing our understanding of their work is special, even as we foist our favorites on our reading friends and relatives.

For those of us who fancy ourselves writers, the relationship is even more complex, as our love of these authors often derives from a perceived (or wished for) artistic kinship or shared sensibility. We see in their work what is possible; they are our silent shadow-mentors, showing us how it can be done. I have parsed Salter's novel of domestic manners, *Light Years*, with an almost Talmudic obsessiveness, so taken was I with the wonderfully consistent and elegiac tone of his prose, so much was I inspired to want to write like him, or at least understand how he did it. I'm a susceptible reader, and I would come away from these sessions in a kind of emulative hypnosis, phrases in his style unfolding in my head for hours. Then the spell would pass and I'd be just me again, writing the way I do, for better or worse. There was only one James Salter.

He was a closet New York Jew (James Horowitz by birth), a West Point man and a fighter pilot during the Korean War, a screenwriter and a filmmaker, a novelist and journalist and memoirist and short story writer. He wrote many of my personal favorites in most of these categories: screenplay (*Downhill Racer*); novel (toss-up between *Solo Faces* and *Light Years*); memoir (*Burning the Days*); short story ("Platinum," from the collection *Last Night*); travel journalism (*There and Then*); even cookbook/memoir (*Life is Meals*, co-authored with his wife Kay). He was, as all the obits say, a writer's writer, which I take to mean, among other things, that only someone who has tried it can fully appreciate how rare and difficult it is to command one's native language to such varied and finely-tuned effect.

Though ecumenical of genre, he was not prolific, certainly not by the standards of an Oates or an Updike or even a Jonathan Franzen. More than twenty years separated *Solo Faces* from his next and last novel (which we suspected it might be), the valedictory *All That Is* (certainly one of the bolder titles in all of literature). One wishes that he had written more, but then he would have been writing something else entirely.

Salter was an immediate descendant of the Hemingway school of alpha-male writers who approached narrative prose as a contact sport. His description of his flying years in his memoir *Burning the Days* and his autobiographical war novel, *The Hunters*, stand as some of the best writing about piloting aircraft since Saint-Exupéry, and *Solo Faces* is unsurpassed in the authenticity of its depiction of mountain climbing. The most beautiful evocations of the joy of skiing that I've ever read are to be found in his nonfiction collection *There and Then*. One imagines that he devoured life in huge masculine gulps and digested it into prose, yet the co-protagonist of *Light Years* is a rather effete, self-absorbed architect, and it is his wife, the elusive, exquisite Nedra, whose inner life is most vividly conveyed.

He lived, as it seems the greats of his generation always did, in France and New York and for a time in Hollywood, but he spent much of his later life in Aspen, CO. Every time I passed through Colorado (usually to ski), I fantasized about looking him up and knocking on his door, just to thank him and shake his hand, maybe ask him where to eat and which runs were good that day. I regret that I never did it, though he probably would have slammed the door in my face; he wanted fame (he as much as said so), but not, I suspect, that kind.

The elusiveness of fame and worldly success is a recurring concern in Salter's writing. Nowhere is the inner man laid bare more starkly than in a passage from *Burning the Days*, in which the first moon landing vaults some of his former pilot colleagues into permanent renown on a summer night when Salter is pursuing mere sex:

> "I have never forgotten that night or its anguish. Pleasure and inconsequence on one hand, immeasurable deeds on the other. I lay awake for a long time thinking of what I had become."

Romantic love as a great distraction from the important things in life is another Salter theme. I believe his view of life's true reward, perhaps its true greatness, lies elsewhere, in family and the love of one's children. His first child, a daughter, died in his arms at age 25. Here is a passage from *Light Years*, written several years earlier:

> "Of them all, it was the true love. Of them all, it was the best. That other, that sumptuous love which made one drunk, which one longed for, envied, believed in, that was not life. It was what life was seeking; it was

a suspension of life. But to be close to a child, for whom one spent everything, whose life was protected and nourished by one's own, to have that child beside one, at peace, was the real, the deepest, the only joy."

One of the pleasures of being an older reader is that you can revisit novels read long ago and experience them in an entirely new way. My encounters with Salter occurred in two widely-separated periods of my reading life; first, when I was in my thirties and discovered *Solo Faces*, his incomparable short novel of an American alpinist in France; *A Sport and a Pastime*, about a young American and his French girlfriend, motoring and ruminating and lovemaking their way through Provence; and *Light Years*, arguably his finest novel, about a couple and their daughters living on the banks of the Hudson, whose separate ambitions to live distinctive lives erode their marriage over decades. I remember finding *Pastime* rather impenetrable at the time, fascinated though I was by all the lyrically-described sex. *Solo Faces* seemed rather leadenly intellectual compared to *The Eiger Sanction*, a thriller involving mountain climbing that was published around the same time. And even though *Light Years* was recognizable even then as Salter's claim to the pantheon of Great American Writers, I thought it too antique in style, not nearly as hip as my beloved Updike.

Some thirty years later, I re-read these books as part of a re-discovery of Salter, brought about when I began to work on a novel of domestic manners and returned to *Light Years*, with its beautifully elegiac depiction of the long, slow disintegration of a blessed and doomed marriage, for inspiration. Stunned by it as I had not been as a younger man, I made a study of everything Salter had ever written, revisiting *Solo Faces* as a reader who had, by then, been in alpine mountains and, more pertinently, been tutored in the ways life thwarts ambition; and revisiting *A Sport and a Pastime* as a reader who cared less about the sex than about the words perfectly chosen to describe it, who could recognize first-hand the uncanny emotional precision with which Salter captured the small towns and countryside and ineffable romanticism of France.

I re-read *Burning the Days*, luxuriating in its period (basically that of my parents), and in Salter's magical ability to conjure immersive atmosphere out of a few exquisite strokes. And in the midst of this binge, during which I read nothing but Salter, not wanting to break the spell of his style, hoping that it would infect mine, came *All That Is*, out of the blue, basically a fictionalized autobiography, long and plotless, episodic and elegiac – an old man's book, looking back, saluting the past from the high promontory of a life fully lived. It was all I could have hoped for from him.

So what do we do when a favorite author dies? Of mine, first Updike passed a few years ago; now James Salter. We go and pull their books from the shelves, finger them fondly, remember where we were in our lives when we first read them, flip through the pages and search for that passage that has never left us; maybe put them back, maybe sit down and read again. If we're writers, we give thanks for what we learned from them, for the spaces in our language that they opened up to us.

If it is true that Salter wished for greater fame than he achieved in life, I would submit to him, if I could, that that is immortality enough.

June 2015

The State of the Novel:
Fates And Furies

• • •

I BLAME CHARLIE ROSE FOR my reading of Lauren Groff's latest novel, *Fates and Furies*. He spent a full half hour interviewing her on his esteemed eponymous talk show one recent night, and I was instantly stricken with a severe case of writer's envy. Here was a young, thirty-something, mildly pretty, slightly cross-eyed woman I had never heard of (though I vaguely recalled the title of her previous novel, *Arcadia*), trading urbane repartee with Charlie (surely the ultimate promotional interview "get") and talking about the repressed "fury" of women with a breezy, assured manner that radiated Ivy League (Amherst, it turns out), bookish privilege, and years of academic writing programs. She'd won the O. Henry Award and the Pushcart Prize and was short-listed for the National Book Award. And more impressive (to me), she got a half hour on *Charlie Rose*, during which she managed to drop the name of James Salter, one of my favorite authors. Had to read her stuff.

Had to read it, if for no other reason than out of sheer generational envy, to see how this kind of blinding literary success was being accomplished by the generation following mine. My wife, also intrigued and a voracious reader, pushed a button, and Amazon (it's true) promptly delivered *Fates and Furies*, with its furiously busy blue cover, to our doorstep.

This is the place to say that as a reader I am tainted not only by generational and vocational envy of younger, successful authors, but by being a writer. I read novels that are close in genre or style to what I might write – hence *Fates* – as an act of reverse engineering: to see how the author did it, the way an auto mechanic might strip an engine. And of course, in the process I'm comparing my own work at fiction (thus far resoundingly unpublished) with what the world has pronounced to be excellence in the form.

So my reading of *Fates* was both annoying and oddly comforting. Annoying because I was once again convinced that what passes for literary excellence these days is a crabbed and shrunken version of what it once was; and comforting because, hey, that's a standard I might meet!

Each half of *Fates and Furies* tells the story of a marriage from the perspective of one of the spouses (and, rather randomly, several other characters, including, briefly and unaccountably, a house cat). This *Rashomon* trope is an annoyance right off the bat, because you know that the author is holding back truths (or, worse, wants you to know there are none), and that of course when you get to the other spouse's point of view you'll find that what you've read in the first half is bunk or delusional or fatally mistaken. This tends to undermine our investment in the narrative and, more importantly, in the protagonists, who are, moreover, startlingly unsympathetic: the husband is a reckless narcissist whose overwhelming charm is proclaimed but never convincingly portrayed, and the wife is a beautiful, vengeful schemer whom we're intended to forgive because she is that supreme figure in women's fiction, the damaged but indomitable survivor.

Nowhere does writerly affectation announce itself more loudly than in the choices of names for a novel's characters, and Groff's are comically literary: Antoinette, Ariel, Mathilde, Chollie, Aurelie, Land. None of these names is found in nature, and for all of them to be in one book screams academic artifice. The couple's dog is named God, for God's sake. One yearns for a Susan or a John, and there is a Sally and a Leo, but of course she must be spelled Sallie and he must be gay and die quickly (he is and does). The critic Anatole Broyard once took James Salter to task for naming the protagonists in *Light Years* (Salter's own marital saga) Nedra and Viri, to which Salter tartly replied, "Come on, *Anatole*?" But Salter was an amateur of exotic appellations next to Groff. The husband in *Fates*, in what would be dismissed as girlish amateurism in someone who hadn't won the Pushcart Prize, is named Lancelot Satterwhite (Lotto for short, doubling down on the cutesy). The wife starts out as Aurelie but becomes Mathilde. Come on, Lauren.

But we sally onward. The novel opens with bad weather (another emblem of amateurism, if only in the unpublished) – "A thick drizzle from the sky..." (where else would drizzle come from?) – and soon presents a fifty-thousand-foot perspective on the couple whose joint and separate lives we will follow for the next four hundred pages: they scurry around in some sand dunes, couple, are in love. They are, of course, stunningly beautiful, the husband soon to become an improbably successful playwright. From within her fussy editorial brackets, with all the subtlety of a traffic cop, the author instructs us to "[Suspend them there, in the mind's eye....We will return to them. For now, he's the one we can't look away from. He is the shining one.]"

This officious intrusion of the authorial voice deserves reflection. In effective third-person narrative, the author, omniscient though she might be, conspires with the reader to paint the scene, conjure the character, visualize the action. A story about others is being told; we are seduced into listening. We *want* to be seduced. If she succeeds, the author disappears into the narrative, allows us to believe we're co-witnesses to something real rather than an audience to the author's performance.

In *Fates*, Groff constantly interposes herself, dictates rather than conspires, like a librarian shushing rambunctious readers in the stacks; it's her way or the highway. Hence all those brackets, where she corrects our misimpressions, directs our attention, deflates our expectations, foreshadows outcomes. She either doesn't trust the reader, or can't help drawing attention to herself. She's not just omniscient, she's fascist. As a result, we resist her; and a reader's no always means no.

The lofty remove of that initial scene sets the vocal tone of the novel: smug, academic, vaguely condescending, writerly, pedantic. In a wink at her fellow English majors, Groff opens an early chapter with a paraphrase of Melville in *Moby-Dick*: "From the sun's seat, after all, humanity is an abstraction." No one you could ever care about names their dog God (though it allows Groff to write wry sentences like "God grumbled at the door, having been banished"), and one suspects that Groff doesn't care for these people either. They and their lives haven't been deeply imagined; they're artifacts, representations of ideas.

From the title on, Groff seems at pains to display her excellent education. There is the godly perspective, that Greek chorus commentary in brackets, a character so minor she needs no name but is nonetheless named Xanthippe, quotes from Shakespeare, a lengthy play-within-the-novel based on Sophocles' *Antigone* (one of many such synopses jarringly dropped into the narrative as signposts, we are to suppose, for Lancelot's advancing genius but which read like warmed-over notes from Groff's playwriting class back at Amherst), and so on. The plays come off as advertisements of the author's own talents ("See what else I could do if I wanted to?") rather than illustrations of her protagonist's tortured brilliance.

Which is not to say that *Fates and Furies* isn't genuinely erudite, clever, for the most part beautifully written, and ultimately (if belatedly) engaging. It is all those things, as well as craftily commercial, despite its constant references to the classics and its other head-fakes toward literary seriousness. At its core, *Fates* is what the publishing biz calls upmarket women's fiction: a well-written novel of doomed love, peppered with sex (some of it mildly kinky, but none of it the least bit erotic because it's described in the same safe, bloodless, arty prose as the rest of the book), limned in reliable clichés (the grasping southern mother, the drunken playwright, the deprived childhood, the kept woman, the dreamy artist-husband who would have come to nothing but for his mercilessly practical wife, the tragic young hipsters in New York City, definitively done thirty years ago in Jay McInerney's *Bright Lights, Big City* and in no need of repetition), and drenched in melodrama (abortion, prostitution, suicide, sterilization, private investigators, abandoned children). It's positively Dickensian. Groff's protagonists embody such extremes (in looks, achievement, neuroses, backgrounds) that they could exist only in soap opera or, well, women's genre fiction. It's to Groff's credit that she manages to make much of this entertaining and plausible, but no one could mistake it for what we used to call literary fiction; the book's pleasures are mostly guilty ones.

I lost what little credulity I'd clung to when Lancelot, wildly famous by this point, makes an unintentionally sexist speech at Stanford and, embarrassed, in despair, and having lost his wallet, proceeds (of all possible choices) to *walk* from Palo Alto back to San Francisco, where the beautiful Mathilde waits in a Nob Hill hotel. Now anyone who has lived in the Bay Area or has even a passing familiarity with it knows that, for reasons having more to do with local infrastructure and topography than distance, walking from Palo Alto to Nob Hill is virtually impossible, let alone in the span of mere hours that our boy Lotto accomplishes it. Was this clumsy riff on the *Odyssey* a sudden lurch into magical realism, however unearned and inconsistent with the rest of the novel, or just a blatant lack of street sense on the author's part, after all her preening erudition on other topics? Whatever it was, it made me want to throw the book across the room.

What's fascinating about all this is that Groff is, undeniably, a wonderful writer. I say this with honest, undiluted envy. Her command of language is deep and sure, she can snap out a simile with the best of them, her descriptive powers are considerable, and her dialogue is believable. What seems to be lacking is heart, or courage, or vulnerability, or even humility; a quality that would soften the mechanistic clanking of her showy prose and allow us to believe in and care about her protagonists. It's too easy to imagine that, in her portrayal of the shallow, self-centered, over-educated coterie of aging hipsters that populate the book, Groff is writing about the life she's lived, in which extraordinary luck of class and genome assumes the guise of merit, and the rewards of that luck have all the momentum of inevitability.

What does the existence and resounding success of *Fates and Furies* tell us about the state of the American novel, and publishing in general? Surely that, because what passes for literary fiction has become a bastard child of the entertainment industry, even the most erudite and potentially serious novelist must become a genre slave and serve up the exotic, the sensational, the palpably unreal. Certainly that, because it's increasingly women who buy books (and who, for that matter, edit, market, publish, and review them), women's fiction, with its deep roots in melodrama, has become the novel's dominant ecosystem. Arguably, that the range of successful fiction writers and their life experiences, formerly rooted in the real working world, has narrowed to the bandwidth of an MFA program in writing. And surely that these forces are crowding out the kind of novel that Updike's and Salter's and Richard Ford's and the late Kent Haruf's reputations were built on: the novel of the sacred everyday, the divine domestic, the luminously quotidian, what Salter called "the glory of certain moments in life," illuminated and made extraordinary not by a quirky, clockwork plot or outlandish characters, but by the author's deep understanding of and compassion for the prosaic lives that we and his characters live.

As a writer, I learned something important from this novel. I'm a defender and, I hope, a practitioner of "good writing," a proponent of character over premise, a lover of metaphor and adjective, cadence and meter, the music of language for its own sake. Like my heroes Updike (to whom all sex scenes in novels owe a lasting debt) and Salter (who, it's been said, could break your heart with a sentence), Groff is utterly proficient at a certain kind of writerly craft, and I should have loved this book. Yet *Fates and Furies* proves that craft is not enough, that you can be brilliant, beautifully educated, wonderfully fluent, know all the tricks of narrative and story structure, be steeped in the canon, and write lyrically, and yet, over four hundred pages, never touch the reader's heart.

February 2016

Welcome to Writer's Hell

• • •

SAY YOU'RE A WRITER. YOU'VE been a small-town journalist or had a freelance article or two published in one of the big metro newspapers. Or maybe you've made a living as a lawyer or a short-order cook or a surgeon or a car salesman, but at heart you're a writer, and always have been: you've been writing since you could hold a crayon, because that's what you're best at.

You've written something that took a long time and a lot of hard work and a significant excavation of your soul, and you're immensely proud of it, because you think it's good. You think it's good with good reason: because you're highly-educated and have read widely and thoughtfully and are in touch with the *zeitgeist* and are not self-delusional (you're certain); it's gone through countless drafts and you may have even had a few of your most honest, least-toadying friends read it, and in comparing this thing you've written – let's say it's a novel — to what's out there and getting published on a daily basis, it's good. It's very good. And you'd like to see it published. In print. By someone other than yourself. Who would pay you for it, edit it, and market it.

What do you do?

You can be realistic, realize that you are one of hundreds of thousands of people with the same wish, save your excellent novel to its cozy file on your computer, and return to more rewarding pursuits, like your day job or playing the tri-state lottery.

Or you can be a hopelessly narcissistic dreamer and follow the current rules of traditional publishing, which we will now review. These are hard and fast rules, mind you, not subject to evasion or elision, unless of course you happen to be a recent immigrant from Pakistan, hold an advanced degree in mathematics from Cambridge, dabble in high-frequency trading on the side, and your ex-roommate's father is on the board at Hachette:

1. **Get a platform.** If you don't know what a platform is, or don't already have one, save your excellent novel to its cozy file on your computer, and return to more rewarding pursuits. If you do have one, make sure it has at least 10,000 followers.
2. **Identify your genre.** If you don't know what genre your novel falls into (or don't know what a genre is), save your excellent novel, etc. There are approximately 112 genres and hybrid genres, so your book must fit one of them (preferably, Dystopian Young Adult). If your novel has the word "Girl" in the title, forget this and proceed immediately to the next step.
3. **Identify an agent.** It's impossible to address publishers directly these days; they are like blue-footed boobies – so close to extinction that it's illegal to disturb them. But there are thousands of agents; much of Manhattan is occupied by them. So buy a copy of the current *Guide to Literary Agents*, further enriching the Writer's Digest subsidiary of F+W Media, Inc., and cross-reference your genre (see above) to the agents who specialize in it. You can shorten this process somewhat by using online agent databases such as QueryTracker, but this is considered cheating. You like books; use them.
4. **Prepare a query letter.** These are sent as the text of an email, not as an attachment or, God forbid, via snail mail, and must be no more than one page long. No cheating with the font. The query letter must, within that one page, describe your novel in a way that will prevent an agent from hitting the "delete" button over which his or her finger is impatiently hovering. This should require no

less than two months of careful revisions. It must be cute, but not too cute. Engaging but not cloying. Deferential but not groveling. Enthusiastic but not bragging. In lieu of sending out dozens of query letters (less than 100 is considered slacking), it's far more authentic and no less effective to attend a pitch-slam at a Writer's Digest conference in some distant city, along with the graduates of the last 10 years of Iowa Writers' Workshops.

5. **Wait**. Some few agents will respond to your query letter within a day or so. Others within two or three months. Most, never. They're too busy, overwhelmed by the sea of queries that washes against their bulwarks daily, and doing their real jobs, which is to try to find publishing homes for the writers they already represent. Or they're out looking for other work. In any event, you won't know which will respond and which will maintain a stony, aloof silence, as though you were the narcissistic, self-deluded dreamer you're beginning to suspect you are. There isn't a law firm in the country that would treat prospective clients like this, but then not nearly as many people want a lawyer as want to see their first novel published, and there are even more lawyers than there are literary agents.

6. **Provide sample pages**. A handful of the hundred or so agents you contact may be sufficiently intrigued by your query, or sufficiently unoccupied with other matters, that they will ask to see the first ten or 20 or 50 pages of your novel, the premise being that if in that span of pages your writing manages to penetrate the carapace of jaded cynicism that has built up over their years of reading fragments of manuscripts, you must be onto something. And if not, not. Never mind that this a little like looking at the bottom left square foot of *Guernica* to determine whether it's worth anything; these are professionals you're dealing with.

7. **Sign a contract with the agent**. Should an agent want to take you on, you will be presented with a legal document assigning to them a significant portion of whatever earnings accrue from your

novel. Needless to say you should read this carefully, and perhaps also have it reviewed by one of those aforementioned law firms, who will be much more interested in your call than the literary agencies you've been slavishly stalking.
8. **Wait.** (See item 5 above, substituting your agent for yourself, and publishers for agents. Adjust probabilities for the fact that the average agent agrees to represent a tiny fraction of books queried, and a major publisher agrees to publish an even tinier fraction of the books whose proposals it receives from agents.)
9. **Sign a contract with a publisher.** Having reached the promised land, you will be presented with a contract with the publisher, granting them extensive rights to your work in exchange for a piteously small amount of money. Needless to say, the law firm referenced in items 5 and 7 should again be consulted.
10. **Go on a book tour.** You know all about this; you've been fantasizing about it for years.
11. **Hear from the publisher** that your book was bought by only 7000 of your 10,000 followers, and that it's been remaindered.

If all this strikes you as bitterly absurd or even insulting, if the industry that exploits the ambitions of aspiring writers strikes you as borderline fraudulent, it might be the time to examine why you want to have your book published in the first place. The writer's vocation has always been a dicey proposition, in which the odds against making a living were long and the chance of fame vanishingly slim. But the current state of traditional print publishing, disfigured by a disastrous confluence of academic writing programs (too many students who have been encouraged to believe themselves to be writers), the internet (too many avenues of expression for this belief), the cult of celebrity (J.K. Rowling-like rags-to-riches stories), and corporate consolidation (too few publishers), has made those odds much longer and the prospect much meaner.

Maybe your motivation is purely commercial; it was either write that novel, or open a pop-up cupcake shop, and the novel required less capital and has a bigger upside (assuming you become the next Hugh Howey). But if you want fame, or to make a lot of money, there are far, far more efficient, less time-consuming, and more probable ways to achieve those things than pursuing print publication. If you presented the above steps to a bunch of venture capitalists as your business plan, they'd throw you out of the room.

I know what you're thinking: you're the exception to the rule. You're the one who will win the publishing lottery against all odds. I know you're thinking this because I think the same thing, and that is the essence of the reason there is no hope for either one of us.

If we stubbornly insist that, no, we really want affirmation *as writers*, we're probably in the grip of a mythology about being an artist that, if we want to get serious about it, would be much better served by a cultivated indifference to fame and money – and to mainstream publishing.

If we write for the sheer joy of writing, let's be writers. Let's be real writers – which is to say artists — and not fodder for an ossified commercial machine that has no reliable means of detecting when and where real art happens, and could care less. Let's take back what was originally ours, which is the joy of self-expression, or of simple storytelling, and forget the business angle. Let's work on improving our craft, not on increasing the followers of our "platforms."

If our lifetime as ardent readers has taught us anything, it's that because something got published means next to nothing about its quality; utter junk is published every day. Our work is no less worthy because it is rejected (or, more likely, never really evaluated), and would be no more worthy if by wild chance you or I won the publishing lottery and it saw print.

How do other artists find expression in the face of their obscurity? Visual artists get their work shown in local galleries, in their friends homes, or on the street. Singers and songwriters perform in local coffee shops and bars, print their own CDs, and find outlets on the internet. What is it about writing that makes us think that only if our work is physically published by a corporation in New York have we achieved anything?

    Writers, be artists. Take back your art and treat it as the inherently valuable work that you believe it to be.

November 2015

Politics

· · ·

The Snowden Muddle

• • •

F. Scott Fitzgerald said that the test of a first-rate intelligence is the ability to hold two opposing ideas in mind at the same time and still retain the ability to function. A lot of us are trying to meet that test in the case of the Snowden leaks and their ongoing repercussions. I for one will confess that from the moment the leaks first surfaced, my ideas – far from first-rate — have been a bit of a muddle, and I suspect that muddle is widely shared regardless of one's position on the political spectrum.

This muddle stems from a conflict between two reactions: on one hand, revulsion at the naiveté, gullibility, and self-righteousness of Snowden himself, at the stupidity of a system that could allow a such a self-aggrandizing drone to come into possession of highly sensitive information, and at the predictably awful consequences of that information's dissemination — the degrading of America's credibility and influence in the world, the compromising of U.S. intelligence capabilities, the likely further balkanization of the internet, etc.

On the other hand, there is an equally strong revulsion at the idea that a bunch of faceless functionaries at the NSA (and elsewhere) could presume, on whatever premise, to invade the privacy of millions of people (including the leaders of allied nations), to collect mountains of personal meta-data for later perusal at whim, to undermine private encryption methods to make us more vulnerable to this prying, to bend private companies to these dubious purposes, and to resort to secret courts for blessing of all this – in short, to personify the fascistic tendencies that our national values supposedly abhor, and that our Constitution prohibits. Much as we might disapprove of the messenger and his methods, the message is of huge significance.

Putting this in political terms, the Snowden case catches liberals between their belief in the good works and trustworthiness of big technology and big government, and their belief in the sanctity of privacy and individual choice. The case catches conservatives between their belief in a strong national defense (which includes espionage) and a powerful executive branch, and their belief in a laissez-faire marketplace, diminished government intervention in private affairs, and an originalist view of the Constitution. (Similar quandaries are raised (or should be) for both factions by, say, the Obama Administration's extensive use of Predator drones, the recent Texas legislation restricting abortions, or the ongoing prosecutions at Guantanamo.)

Conservatives and liberals alike can agree that Snowden is at best a product of profoundly stupid government subcontracting, and at worst a traitor, without necessarily agreeing on whether public awareness of the NSA's activities is a bad thing, or what if anything to do about them. Would that we could put the genie of that awareness back in the bottle, but we can't, and had Snowden and *The Guardian* not colluded to out the NSA, the fact of this sort of activity would have emerged eventually by some other means. The very technology that enables this sort of wholesale snooping also eliminates the possibility of wholesale secrecy.

Now that we know at least a bit of what is going on, it seems incumbent on us as citizens to insist that the NSA, CIA, etc. be accountable for their actions under the rule of law, including Constitutional law. "Trust us" is not enough. The Constitution's prohibition of unreasonable searches and seizures is unequivocal, and it has yet to be convincingly shown why the NSA's global dragnet techniques are reasonable.

To properly inform the debate may require further disclosure of what our government has been up to, and the question will then be, disclosure to whom? Perhaps there is a workable proxy for the voting public in this regard, but recent performance of our representatives in Congress suggests that they are not it. Few of us truly understand the internet itself and, with all due respect to Diane Feinstein, that includes most elected officials. Should we accept the decisions of the Foreign Intelligence Surveillance Court, which gives license to much of the NSA's internet-trolling activities? Hard to tell, since its deliberations and rulings are secret. What are the limits of what is possible in terms of internet surveillance, and how does one define the boundaries, within those limits, of what is needed to save lives from future terrorism? The questions require not just wise jurists, but first-rate hackers to answer. Politicians fall into neither category.

As we try to find a way out of this muddle, we must not lose sight of the forest of Constitutional concerns in the trees of nationalism. The decades-old legislation that gave rise to this system of secret, parallel government needs to be reexamined, and the age-old tradeoff between security and liberty needs to be openly debated in the light of 21st century technology, informed by people who truly understand both.

November 2013

What is Terrorism?

• • •

THE RECENT ATROCITIES IN PARIS and San Bernardino have ratcheted up our collective anxiety about international terrorism, and rightly so. But what exactly are we talking about when talk about terrorism? Much is made of President Obama's supposed refusal to "call Islamic terrorism by its name." The word terrorism itself has become generalized, its meaning expanded to encompass sets of beliefs rather than objective criteria.

In our haste to assign blame and defend ourselves, we risk confusing terrorism with simple crime, and that confusion itself poses risks. All terrorism is criminal, but only some crimes constitute terrorism. Especially when emotions and the pressure to react to them are high, we need to think clearly about the varieties of physical threat to our communities and ourselves, how terrorism differs from simple crime, and how we should deal with each of them.

At one end of the spectrum is Paris, where a group of organized, ideologically-motivated, and remotely-directed thugs engaged in random acts of lethal violence. That scenario is as concrete an example of terrorism as we're likely to come up with. The ultimate template for this sort of thing is, of course, 9/11, and its identifying elements are (a) coordination among multiple participants, (b) external direction of the group, including but not limited to direction across national borders, (c) ideological (as contrasted with economic or personal) motivation, and (d) mass killings.

At the other end of the spectrum of public violence is Columbine, and Sandy Hook, and Aurora, and the Washington Navy Yard shootings, the shooting in Tuscon of Gabrielle Giffords, and for that matter the attempt on Ronald Reagan's life, where deranged individuals, acting alone (though often abetted by the ready availability of automatic weapons), and motivated primarily by their own inner demons, wreak lethal havoc. Of the above indicia of terrorism, all but the use of extreme violence are missing in these cases. These are simple though abhorrent crimes, often committed by the certifiably insane and, in the modern world where instruments of mass death can be bought over the counter, mostly unpreventable.

Somewhere in the middle are the cases of the Boston bombers, the Planned Parenthood shooter, the Fort Hood shooter, the Oklahoma City bomber and, most recently, the San Bernardino shootings, where the actors may assume a quasi-military bent, may spout a religious phrase in the act of killing or later claim to be motivated by an ideology, but who acted without external direction and whose claims to ideological motivation may be so thoroughly mixed with their individual pathologies as to make them moot. Are they terrorists, or merely criminals? When someone is "inspired" by, but unknown to, a foreign organization like ISIS, does their crime become terrorism, any more than the violent act of a teenage boy who has been inspired by a video game?

Right-wing indignation over Obama's hesitancy to label San Bernardino as an instance of Islamic terrorism is instructive. The terrorist label is useful to some because it simplifies complex facts and presumes an external enemy against whom war can at least theoretically be waged. It suggests the possibility of retribution, or of prevention through ever-greater infringements on our freedoms, rather than the moral slog required of us by the randomness of pathology and personal evil. It shifts the narrative away from the political and economic forces that sanctify gun possession, underfund the treatment of mental illness, support the medieval value systems of places like Saudi Arabia, or perpetuate the social conditions that give root to jihadist propaganda.

Obama's opponents manage to sound indignant that the question of gun control has even been raised in the context of mass shootings, as though it represents an unwillingness to confront the threat of Islamic jihadism. But there is nothing mutually exclusive about wanting to defeat religious extremists and wanting to deprive them and other psychopaths of weaponry wherever possible.

Calling criminals terrorists elevates them above their station, gives them media time we would never confer on simple thugs, and relieves us of the obligation to address our own complicity in the violence we fear. The terrorist label too often legitimizes religious bigotry and lends an unwarranted dignity to simple, inexcusable crime. We should use it sparingly, and with a technical precision that reflects our seriousness in bringing actual terrorists to justice.

December 2015

Why is "Liberal" a Dirty Word?

• • •

IN THE RELATIVELY SHORT SPAN of my adult life (I attended college in the 1970s), the word "liberal," used in its political sense, has gone from being a badge of widely-shared, almost consensus values — the innocuous sibling of "conservative," the natural flip-side of the national political consciousness – to being a virtual obscenity, one that invites such vitriol that even certifiable liberals, like Hillary Clinton, refuse to identify with the term, preferring the more ambiguous "progressive" to define her politics. How and why did this happen, and what can be done to rehabilitate a label that, if no longer proudly borne, is at least descriptively useful?

The transformation of "liberal" from rallying cry to epithet is a uniquely American phenomenon having to do, in part, with the predictably pendular swings in voter sympathies between center-left (Johnson, Carter, Clinton, Obama) and center-right (Nixon, Reagan, Bush I, Bush II) and now beyond, into the hard-right fringes staked out by Cruz and Trump and Rubio, where even the most reasonable regulation of firearms is cast as a threat to fundamental liberty, Planned Parenthood is a front for murderers, immigration is a siege on national integrity, diplomacy is "feckless," avoidance of military conflict is cowardly, and every public need should be met by private enterprise or not at all.

Much of this is seasonal political rhetoric that will be corrected when the electoral debate goes national, but it has usurped mainstream media attention to a degree and for so long that much of it seems less bizarre than it would have just a few years ago. The attitudes underlying this rhetoric have seeped into the national consciousness, like lead leaching into drinking water. Liberals, because they are liberals, are taking most of this lying down, and one result is that the label that comfortably defined them for decades has been drained of its meaning and turned into a slur.

Conservatives need to be reminded that liberals were the original opponents of big government. Today's liberalism is a descendant of the Enlightenment philosophy espoused by the anti-monarchists of the 17th century, epitomized by John Locke, who foresaw that dynastic succession, theocratic government, and the divine right of kings were bankrupt, insupportable notions that would be swept away by science, rationalism, and the recognition of universal, "natural" rights, such as equality, freedom of conscience and religion, and of an inherent human dignity superior to and independent of any government. Our Declaration of Independence is a pragmatic expression of this philosophy, and most Americans are, at least in this historical sense, quintessential liberals.

I can't think of Franklin Delano Roosevelt, the father of modern American liberalism, without thinking of my own father, who could barely speak Roosevelt's name without spitting. My father's hatred for Roosevelt was always a bit of a mystery to me, but long after his death I've come to understand that it was more than just the ideological distaste of a life-long Republican for the patrician Democrat who ran the country for an unprecedented four terms when my father was a young man. It was also the product of a deep anxiety, born from his experience of an entire society suddenly and profoundly reshaped, in the midst of war and economic crisis, by the singular hand of the federal government. That much of what resulted was welcome and just (including my father's Social Security checks) was, to my father, largely beside the point; the government had shown what it could do when the people were weak and in disarray, and that power frightened him.

Today's Tea Party Republicans are motivated by a similar fear, or so they say: the feds will come and take our guns, take our wealth and waste it, take our religion and suppress it, take our tribes and deracinate them, take our emblems of individual and national identity and homogenize them. The liberals who run the federal government believe they know better than the common man, and if they have their way, we will cease to be who we are, so we must stop them, bleed them of funding, send the bureaucrats home to more useful pursuits, reinvent the world as we think we once knew it, when lines of class and race and religion and sexual orientation and nationality were deep and clear.

Liberals are the enemy because they promote the Rooseveltian model of a strong central government. Liberals are the enemy because they are defenders of the tawdry secularism that these days passes for culture. Liberals are the enemy because they are too blindly in love with an idea of equality that tends to exempt the individual from responsibility and shift it to the state. Liberals are the enemy because they don't embrace the idea of American exceptionalism any more than their 17th-century precursors accepted the idea of the divine right of kings.

So "liberal" has become a dirty word. And so dearly do liberals hold civil liberties that they accept the vitriol directed at them as one of the inalienable rights of their fellow citizens. This occasionally makes them look like chumps or punching bags, and allows their opponents to dictate even the language – and labels – by which political debate is conducted.

But liberals know that conservatives' animus is misdirected or contrived, that a true liberal stands for individual liberty and responsibility above all else, that what really separates us from our conservative counterparts is not philosophy, but policy. It's no coincidence that "liberty," "liberal" and "libertarian" are so close in etymology, and that liberals and libertarians see eye-to-eye on many issues (an aversion to foreign adventurism among them). The difference is that a liberal sees no threat to individualism in the pursuit of communal improvement through government, while today's hard right sees them as mutually exclusive.

The immoderate, divisive conservatism of Cruz and Trump and Rubio is an expression of resentment at the fact that democracy itself isn't working out the way it did when only some classes and races and genders could vote. Their premise is that we'd rather have a hobbled government or no government than a government of, by, and for the people we don't agree with.

Liberals, on the other hand, know that disagreement and division over policy come with the territory in an inclusive democracy, and prefer persuasion to demolition as a political tool.

Charges of elitism or paternalism notwithstanding, liberals' real sin in the eyes of the hard right is that they haven't given up on the system. They continue to believe that representative democracy, and the centralized government that is its inevitable expression in a continental republic, not only can be made to work, but is the last hope of the modern world for the enduring liberal values that were the motto of the French Revolution and that most Americans still cherish: liberty, equality, fraternity.

Liberals need to reclaim a political language that openly and proudly reflects those values.

Meanwhile, call me a liberal any time. I'll take it as a compliment.

February 2016

"Lucifer in the Flesh": Is Ted Cruz the Antichrist?

• • •

I'M AS AMAZED AND ENTERTAINED as anyone by the gaudy clown car that the Republican Party has become in this election cycle, careening madly between farce and fiasco on its way to this summer's big-top circus in Cleveland. Jeb Bush kicked to the curb, Marco Rubio stuck on repeat, Trump reassuring us of the size of his schwantz, declaring himself shocked – shocked!—to find that a primary system brought to us by the same people who made voter suppression a moral cause is "rigged"; Ted Cruz revealing that because he apparently lets his very young daughters go into public restrooms alone, he doesn't want any guys in there, especially ones who believe they are women; grown men dissing one another's wives and whining that the other guy started it; and poor Kasich, like a substitute teacher in a roomful of delinquents, waving his arms and trying to get someone to pay attention to him. You couldn't make this stuff up.

But then John Boehner, former Speaker of the House, injected a theological consideration into these riveting proceedings, calling Ted Cruz "Lucifer in the flesh." Which finally makes the question unavoidable to the thoughtful voter: is Ted Cruz the Antichrist?

I spent several of my formative years in the company – and to some degree under the influence – of evangelical Christians, the very group of conservatives to whom Ted Cruz pitches himself most strenuously. Of the many Biblical concepts at the heart of evangelical doctrine, the idea of the Antichrist is one of the most important, both because it unites the Pentecostal belief in the end-of-times with every conservative Christian's self-image as a member of a persecuted remnant, and because it intersects with the secular world of politics.

The story of the Antichrist that evangelical Christians distill from various sources in the New Testament (primarily the Books of John, Thessalonians, and especially Revelations) is essentially this: before the Second Coming – the ultimate endgame of Christian theology — can occur, there will rise up a powerful, charismatic figure, human in appearance but in fact the Antichrist, the alter ego of Satan, who will lead the world astray and ultimately into a conflagration (expected by most evangelicals to be nuclear and to be played out in the Middle East) that will only end when Christ returns to call his faithful home to heaven, cast down the Antichrist, and begin his eternal reign on Earth. There are variations on this story, some popularized in the *Left Behind* series of evangelical thriller novels, but that's essentially it (and it's certainly enough).

Key to this narrative is the premise that the world will not recognize the Antichrist when he appears. He will not declare himself, lest he have no followers. He will wrap himself in honorific symbols – the U.S. Constitution, say – and deceive even the faithful. He may even claim to be a Christian, and if he does, you can be sure that he will claim to be a better Christian than you and me. He will present himself as a savior. He will be aggressively militaristic, the sort of leader who wouldn't hesitate to "make the sand glow." He may not even *know* that he's the Antichrist, which would enhance his deceptiveness considerably.

It's a given to most evangelicals that, when he appears, the Antichrist will be a politician. How else would he gain access to the levers of power necessary to bring on the end of the world? Where else but in the bowels of godless political institutions – the U.S. Senate, say – would he hone his rhetorical skills to the requisite sliminess? In what other profession is mendacity and ruthlessness so fulsomely rewarded?

I'm going with Boehner. My nomination for Antichrist this election cycle is Ted Cruz, hands down. There's all the vainglory, bombast, and weaseliness that one would expect in an Antichrist, combined with that one perversity no true Antichrist should lack: deeply prideful religiosity, an unctuous sanctimony that requires his constant, gratuitous mention of his own prayerfulness. He even looks like some 18th century cartoonist's vision of the Antichrist, all squint-eyed and pock-marked and pointy-nosed. But let's not get petty.

Given their extensive familiarity with the concept of the Antichrist, one would expect that evangelical Christians would be uniquely well-positioned to sniff out potential Antichrists when they appear. How then, if my and John Boehner's suspicion that Ted Cruz is the Antichrist holds any water, can one explain Cruz's popularity with evangelicals? To ask the question is to vastly underestimate the political and theological sophistication of evangelicals. If you long for the final resolution of history in the Second Coming and believe that the Antichrist must arise before that can happen, who else would you vote for?

April 2016

Lawmaking Is Not Binary

• • •

THE CURRENT OUTCRY OVER THE barely-functioning Obamacare website is a carnival sideshow, and like any carnival, will pass. But once the online experience is improved, and the actuarial realities of how citizens make their health insurance choices are assessed, we will be left with a law on the books that Republicans and Democrats alike will undoubtedly want to amend. That process, and not repeal or obstruction, is what is owed the American people.

The Affordable Care Act is intended to accomplish the enormously difficult task of reforming the existing system of health insurance in ways that address both its demographic and geographic inequities: distortions in the allocation of health care risks and costs arising from the fact that some are insured while others are not, and distortions in the availability of coverage under a crazy quilt of state-level regulation and corporate profit-seeking. This is, as they say in Washington, a "heavy lift," and it is not particularly surprising that these earliest days of its implementation have been rough going.

So far, what we are getting from Republicans is barely-concealed delight in what they dearly wish the American people to perceive as an abject failure. What we are getting from Democrats is defensive downplaying of what is, at minimum, a disastrous product roll-out that may mask deeper flaws. Lost in this orgy of *schadenfreude* and breast-beating is the harder task for Republicans: shouldering some share of the burden of lawmaking, which means proposing legislative fixes to what they claim is broken.

Democrats likewise need to acknowledge that it would be almost impossible for this immense slug of legislation to be fair and functional in all respects, and that it will undoubtedly need to be amended, perhaps repeatedly, before it works well enough.

At the fringe, of course, are those who think that the very idea of a law administering the availability of health care is another step on the slippery slope to Fabian socialism. For them, nothing short of the repeal of Obamacare (and for some, secession from the Union) will suffice. But for the rest of our elected representatives, who surely must still be in the majority, a more rational and humane health care system is a legitimate object of federal legislation, just as is a strong military or a safe food supply. For them, the Affordable Care Act should represent, if not an apotheosis of legislative wisdom, at least a first step toward an end that their constituents deserve.

Complex and arguably coercive though the ACA may be, it is far less so than another piece of unpopular legislation that we have nonetheless lived with for about a hundred years, and that has undergone countless fixes over its lifetime in an effort to address another unfortunate necessity: taxation. I refer, of course, to the Internal Revenue Code. Originally enacted in 1926, reviled as in need of "reform" for most of its existence, the Code (as its aficionados fondly call it) has been amended countless times, and has famously ballooned from a relatively modest few provisions into almost ten thousand "sections," each dealing with a separate detail of the taxation of our lives, our ways of making money, and our deaths. As a young tax lawyer in the 1970s, I and my mentors knew it as the Internal Revenue Code of 1954, in reference to its then-last major overhaul. Since then Congress has passed an average of at least one tax bill each year, including another major overhaul in 1986. For better or worse, the Code is a living piece of legislation, and it is safe to say it will never truly be finished.

To be sure, much of this continuous change is the result of the seamier side of lawmaking: lobbyists and ideologues have had their way with the Code since its inception, and much of its complexity is owed to the range of special interests – often contradictory – being served in its arcane provisions. But the evolution of the Code is also a function of periodic collaborative efforts by both parties to get the unfortunate necessity of taxation right – to make it more in tune with what is really going on in the world, more efficient, more understandable, more fair.

Contrast this long analog history of legislative work with the starkly binary approach of today's Tea Party Republicans to the unfortunate necessity of health care: Obamacare is flawed; therefore it must be repealed or, when that fails, "de-funded" (as the latter can be achieved by sheer gridlock). But responsible lawmaking is not binary, not a world of simple yes or no; it is iterative, the product of reciprocity, repeated tries and – dare we use the word? – compromise. A statute is not a unitary object that must be enacted or repealed *in toto*; it is a weave of provisions of inevitably varying sense and effectiveness, always subject to further refinement through amendment.

Republicans would like to paint Obamacare as an executive fiat issued by the man whose name it bears, when of course it is nothing of the sort. It is a piece of undoubtedly flawed legislation, duly passed by a duly-elected Congress. It's not just the privilege, but the duty of our lawmakers – Republicans and Democrats alike – to get about the hard work of improving it until it best serves the people who elected them.

November 2013

Politics and the War of Values

• • •

IN THIS VERY STRANGE ELECTION cycle, pundits and politicians alike are at pains to explain the cause of its strangeness, and most have concluded that it is the anger of the American people at the political establishment and the status quo of government that accounts for the astonishing inability of the Republican Party to offer a plausible nominee for the presidency, the weirdly persistent appeal of Bernie Sanders' repackaged socialism to millions of millennials, and the bored cynicism with which Hillary Clinton's inevitable candidacy has been greeted.

By these accounts, the voters' anger is rooted in the economy and its overly leisurely recovery from the biggest financial meltdown since the Great Depression. On the right, the hope is that Trump's vulgar egocentrism can destabilize the status quo and deliver us back to a halcyon if mythological past where every able-bodied man or woman could get a good job and America threw its military weight around with well-intentioned abandon. On the left, the hope is that Sanders' warmed-over populism and cranky hectoring could shame the elites into bestowing still greater entitlements on the multitudes, the national debt be damned. And Clinton – poor centrist Hillary – occupies that awful twilight world of old-school politics, where all she can offer is a pallid incrementalism, and no one has the patience for that.

None of this accounts adequately for our current plight, however. The bizarre political landscape that we've created has deeper roots than mere economic discontent. Those roots reach down into the culture wars that have dogged American politics for more than a generation, in which two large factions of the voting public have gone their separate ways, never to be reunited by mere politics.

Forget right and left, liberal and conservative, with all the baggage those labels bring with them. The division in the body politic springs from two fundamentally different value systems.

On one hand we have Rationalists, who believe that, whatever awaits us after death, here in the present we have only ourselves to blame for most of our predicaments, and only ourselves to rely on for solutions to them. These voters, while they may be regular churchgoers, are deeply pragmatic and thoroughly secular in their view of policy issues, and hence measure them by the criterion expressed by the English philosopher Jeremy Bentham: what will produce the greatest good for the greatest number? Communal good takes precedence over individual whim or personal belief in these voters' view. Anything that stands in the way of solving a communal problem – religious doctrine, tradition, individual eccentricity – is held suspect by these voters and must justify itself on the grounds of rational pragmatism, not absolutist belief. Rationalists are skeptical even of historical precedent, believing with Emerson that "no man will read history aright who thinks that what was done in a remote age, by men whose names have resounded far, has any deeper sense than what he is doing today." Hence, rather than deify the Founding Fathers, they take the Constitution with a grain of salt, as the work of men of their time and place.

Rationalist voters are activist rather than fatalist, relativist rather than absolutist. They believe human experience to be malleable rather than preordained. They are communal rather than tribal, globalists rather than nationalists. They cherish individual liberty up to the point where it infringes on the well-being of the next person, and they see the work of government as a continual balancing of individual liberty against the goal of the greatest good for the greatest number.

What these values boil down to in policy terms is that Rationalists favor gun control but don't mind gay marriage; they oppose capital punishment but not abortion; they see the need for tax regimes that burden people proportionally with their means, and for communal amelioration of individual misfortune and stupidity; they recognize that a continental republic requires a "big government," but want it to remain solvent; they are skeptical of the efficacy of military force and sympathetic to diplomacy; they find patriotism beside the point and moralism a distraction from work that needs to be done.

On the other hand we have Spiritualists, who believe that God or nature has already dictated the answers to most of the policy questions of the day, that individual action, albeit pre-ordained, determines human endeavor, and that the past is always prelude. They believe in a natural law that supersedes human law and operates regardless of Bentham's criterion of the greatest good for the greatest number. In these voters' view, individual preference, guided by these higher principles, must always take precedence over the collective good, because they believe that out of the exercise of those individual rights will emerge a good yet higher than what any government could devise.

They are fatalist rather than activist, absolutist rather than relativist, tribal rather than communal. Many social problems are inherent in the human condition, they believe, and to try to ameliorate them is wasteful or counterproductive. They see the Founding Fathers as secular saints and the Constitution as sacred text. They see the work of government as the promotion and protection of individual freedom.

Hence, in policy terms, Spiritualists oppose gun control and believe that God forbids gay marriage and abortion but, being vengeful, permits capital punishment. They regard homosexuality and transsexuality as a denial of nature and God's plan. They regard big government as an inherent threat to individual liberty, and hence to the collective good that they believe will spring naturally from its exercise. For them, taxes are always too high, as they infringe on individual liberty, and they are always too progressive, because they believe that individual economic success should be rewarded, not penalized. They project tribalism from the personal to the national, and hence are ardent patriots and proponents of American exceptionalism and military intervention.

What could possibly resolve these two points of view? Their debate is as old as the Enlightenment.

Take the recent litigation brought by an order of nuns called the Little Sisters of the Poor (was ever a plaintiff more sympathetically named?), challenging *not* the requirement of the Affordable Care Act that employee insurance plans cover contraceptive drugs, including certain abortifacients, but the *exception* to that requirement already provided to employers with religious scruples about it, such as the Sisters. This exception allows such employers to "opt-out" and cause a third party to provide the mandated insurance coverage for contraceptives. But the Sisters complain that even filling out the form required to opt out makes them complicit in delivering contraceptives to their employees, which offends their religious beliefs and – more important from a legal perspective – unduly burdens their free exercise of religion under the Constitution and the Religious Freedom Restoration Act of 1993 (a law with a fascinating history stemming from a case in which Native Americans were prevented from being employed because they'd used peyote in their religious rituals).

Needless to say, the Spiritualists among us side with the Little Sisters on this point, and the Rationalists stand in awe that anyone would spend the time and money to fight over such things. (One can imagine the meeting in which someone else's lawyers explained to the Little Sisters why they should be outraged by the ACA's opt-out procedure.) No one, after all, is requiring the Little Sisters to have an open bin of birth control pills in their convent, nor that they inform or encourage their employees about contraception. The issue is whether their employees who obviously don't share the Sisters' religious scruples and *want* contraceptives will have them covered by insurance, or whether they will have to jump through additional hoops to obtain them. This is spiritualism of a very high order. The employees in question will no doubt exercise their individual choice on the matter regardless of the Sisters' position, or they already adhere to the Sisters' doctrinal views, in which case the issue is moot. If individual choice is the ultimate good, let it rule, say the Rationalists. Do your work as missionaries of the Church and convert those contraceptive-popping employees to good Catholic doctrine, don't waste your time in courtrooms parsing the degrees of your doctrinal purity.

Spiritualist views similarly animate recent accounts of bakeries and other establishments refusing to provide cakes and other accoutrements for gay weddings on the grounds that such refusal is an expression of the proprietor's religion. Rationalists ask: In what possible way is a commercial transaction, in which an object is sold by one person to another in a place open to the public for that purpose, an expression of religious belief? If the gay couple in question wanted to buy a wedding cake to throw it against a wall, would that have compromised the proprietor's beliefs? Presumably not, yet this suggests that religious merchants should be engaging in far more due diligence into their customers' intentions for their products than is currently the norm. Rationalists would welcome this sort of scrutiny to be applied to, say, gun sales. But bakeries? Rationalists say: do your thing with intention and love, then let it go and let others do theirs. No harm, no foul. (All sports fans are Rationalists.) Spiritualists say: your desires take the back seat to my beliefs, and you must allow me to act out their consequences even if those consequences conflict with your desires.

Take also the recent kerfuffle over a North Carolina law that, in addition to overturning previously legislated anti-discrimination protections for LGBT people, requires that in government buildings individuals may only use restrooms that correspond to their birth gender. One of the arguments put forth in defense of this law is that little girls might be preyed upon in bathrooms by adult men pretending for the occasion to be women. Leave aside the questions of how such a law is to be enforced, or why a gradeschool girl (or boy, for that matter) would be alone in a public restroom in the first place. Are there any known instances of these bathroom sex predators in drag? None that can be cited (though the hypothetical suggests possible pathology on the part of those posing it). So it comes down to the belief that transgender persons are an affront to a higher law, one that can't be legislated but whose consequences perhaps can be. Rationalists see this as a pointless fight over a non-problem; Spiritualists see it as a symbolic defense of a cherished norm.

Then there is the issue of gun control, which the recent atrocity in Orlando has once again brought to the fore. Rationalists see this as a relatively simple question of limiting access to military-grade weaponry for the protection of the public. Spiritualists see the right of an individual to own a gun — no matter its grade or purpose - as a Constitutional absolute that must not be infringed in any degree, presumably as a hedge against some imagined scenario where that individual might wish to rise up against his government. For Rationalists, a gun is a dangerous object, like a car or an amphetamine, whose ownership and use we regulate. For Spiritualists, a gun is an emblem of individual freedom, untouchable as religion.

Is there a politician on the horizon who has a hope of reconciling these disparate world views? Not currently. Trump falls outside either belief system, making it up as he goes along. Hillary is a thorough Rationalist who can only offend Spiritualist standards. She will likely win, but only because Rationalists tend to congregate on the coasts, where the Electoral College assigns the most votes. For a bit longer, we will probably remain a politically Rationalist nation, but the underlying schism in values will remain.

June 2016

Easy Targets: The Fun and Futility of Anti-Trump Journalism

• • •

IN THIS SILLY SEASON FOR American politics, I read daily a respectable smattering of serious journalism about Donald Trump, the now more-than-presumptive Republican nominee for the presidency of the United States. I read, daily, the Wall Street Journal op-ed pages, where the stable of staunchly right-wing regulars ranges from Bret Stephens, a conservative think-tanker who is philosophically appalled and personally offended (as he often is) by the Trump candidacy, and who bluntly calls him a "sociopath," to Carl Rove, perennial Republican apparatchik and aspiring Porky Pig impersonator, who offers panicky corrective exhortations to the wayward, self-satisfied, seemingly ad hoc Trump campaign.

I also read the New Yorker, which in its pages and online has unleashed an unremitting fusillade of passionately literate anti-Trump material, from Adam Gopnik's anguished calls to understand Trump as a harbinger of pure fascism, to Jane Mayer's methodically incendiary piece on Tony Schwartz, the repentant ghostwriter of Trump's own Mein Kampf, "The Art of the Deal," in which Schwartz describes Trump as a ruthless narcissist whose election would create "an excellent possibility that it will lead to the end of civilization" (not to put too fine a point on it); to Lauren Collins' deadpan dissection of Melania Trump; to Amy Davidson's sanguinely trenchant daily reportage from the floor of the Republican National Convention

This is all a heck of a lot of fun for your average centrist political news junkie, but does it move any needles? It has the feel of an echo chamber, a self-reinforcing media feedback loop, which we've each managed to construct for ourselves, in which the already-converted preach eloquently to each other and no one else listens. I find myself, like any good liberal, eagerly consuming anti-Trump journalism, whether emanating from the right or left, like candy: it's abundant, it goes down easy, you want more. But after a while it starts to make you nauseous.

This isn't the nausea that comes from a dire recognition of the spot we've gotten ourselves into as a nation. Rather, it's the nausea of excessive self-indulgence. Adam Gopnik touched on this briefly in a recent piece when he noted that "while the habits of hatred get the better of the right, the habits of self-approval through the fiction of being above it all contaminate the center."

I'm old enough to have been aware of Donald Trump for several decades, and for some of those years as a resident of New York City, where he was an ongoing joke long before his goofy self-caricature on "The Apprentice": the kid of a local real estate mogul throwing his money around, womanizing, serially bankrupt, serially reinvented, but consistently self-promoting in a comically obvious, ham-handed way, like the ads for kitchen implements on late-night TV, or a wannabe Hugh Hefner. If you paid attention to him at all, it was with the nearly universal condescension that New Yorkers bestow on pretenders and neophytes. He was the harbinger of an era when unbridled narcissism could pass for a profession rather than a pathology. It was impossible to take him seriously.

Now we must. Not the man himself, of course, but what he represents and the risks that it poses to the republic: a hate-baiting indifference to fact and nuance posing as candor, a disdain for civil discourse, a blinding self-absorption posing as personal strength. It's not that he's evil; no one who's watched his career unfold thinks he's much worse than a boor. It's simply that he is utterly unqualified for the post he's seeking.

But enough with the piling-on of anti-Trump rhetoric, the reaching for new metaphors in an effort to capture the tawdry essence of what his candidacy tells us about ourselves and our politics. No one's going to be persuaded one way or the other by the next story about Trump's treatment of women, his companies' bankruptcies, his yet-to-be-uttered, inevitable insults and falsehoods. We get it. Conservatives get it. This is easy. We need to return Trump to his natural habitat of real estate deals and cheap celebrity, and elect grown-ups with plausible backgrounds to represent us in government. We need to mark this down as a remarkable if sporadically entertaining aberration in our national life, and move on.

To do that, we must discard "the fiction of being above it all," stop enjoying the anti-Trump diatribes and gloating over his serial gaffes. We must escape a media narrative that, inadvertently or deliberately, tends to normalize the extreme abnormality of what we're witnessing: a thoroughly unprepared man to whom consensus is an alien notion, with no experience in elected office or in representing anyone but himself, offered up as the Republican Party's nominee for the presidency of the most powerful nation on earth.

We must, above all, vote this November, and urge our fellow citizens to vote, rather than sit this one out because one dislikes Hillary only slightly less than Donald. This is not the time for prissy ideological purity or disdain for the entire political process; a pox on both houses will surely be a pox on us all.

Trump is an easy target, and the tsunami of anti-Trump journalism is loads of fun for most of us. But from here on out, the ballot is the only statement about Trump that matters.

July 2016

Society

· · ·

Can We Talk About the Fatwagons?

• • •

CAN WE TALK ABOUT THE fatwagons? Can we? You know what I mean; they go by various helpful-sounding names like "mobility chair," "power chair," or the ubiquitously advertised "Hoveround"(tm). They are present-day versions of those flying couches that the morbidly obese earthlings of the future were eventually convinced to dispense with in the endearing Pixar movie, *WALL-E*.

I call them fatwagons because, as in the movie, the people you mainly see in them are (deep breath) fat. (Sorry about that word, "fat," but it's succinct and to the point.) Not just a little fat. Not just "overweight." Really fat. Morbidly obese, like those folks in the future. But this is now.

And they are suddenly everywhere. Recently, in the local supermarket, a veritable squadron of these chairs and their riders arrived and began hungrily cruising the aisles. I wondered if the chairs were street-legal or if they'd been offloaded from some humongous, specially-designed van with the carbon footprint of a locomotive.

Am I alone in seeing deep irony in a really fat person riding in a motorized chair? How about a really fat person in a motorized chair making selections in the pastry section of Whole Foods? Yes, she *may* have been buying that German chocolate cake for her niece's birthday party, but from the lustful look on her face I somehow doubt it. Does the phrase "downward spiral" have any relevance here? What is the thinking behind this? I'm trying to imagine the dialogue:

"Doctor, I'm really having trouble walking."
"Hmm. That could be because you're morbidly obese."
"Is there anything you can do, Doctor?"
"Well, let's see. I can prescribe a motorized chair so you don't have to walk at all."

Hopefully this conversation never actually occurs, as it's just a tiny bit like recommending that an alcoholic live *directly* next to a bar to avoid the pain of getting even slightly sober, or that we deal with poverty by eliminating welfare programs.

But maybe that conversation does occur, because it's the product of a sick symbiosis between the patient's inability to stop eating and get some exercise, and a medical system that throws machinery at every problem at the expense of the general public. What do you think a Hoveround(tm) costs? When you look on their website to find out, you'll see that you shouldn't worry your fat head about it, because Medicare will pay for it.

I know, I know. I'm a naturally thin person with no idea of the struggles that overweight people go through, a bigot pure and simple – I'm a fatist. I'm sure I need to work on this. Some fat people are fat because they have *glandular* disorders, not because they can't imagine passing a day without washing down a few Whoppers with a supersized Coke while lolling about watching Oprah. Some fat people just can't help being fat, and the resulting unavoidable fatness has given them *joint issues*, making it hard or even dangerous for them to walk and requiring the motorized chair.

Let's stipulate that there is a population of motorized chair users out there who simply have no alternative. I am willing to have my taxes help pay for their mobility. But I have the strong suspicion – perhaps based on my fatist bias, I'll admit – that there is another population for whom the motorized chair is just another step in a long journey that began when they were in high school and looked down one day and said "hey, I'm getting a little chubby," but rather than put down the supersized Coke and head for the gym, instead finished it off, ordered another, and found in a few more years that they couldn't see their feet, and began rationalizing that a lot of their friends were putting on weight, too, and that in some cultures having a large belly is a sign of prosperity and wisdom, and that Oprah has weight issues too, and that food addiction is an *addiction*, and that if worst came to worst there was always stomach stapling rather than deny oneself the caloric bounty and sedentary lifestyle that is our right as Americans, and so on up to that moment when the idea of walking began to seem a bit tiresome and a motorized chair a merely rational medical alternative that someone else would pay for.

And it is to that latter population that I say: of *course* your joints are shot; they were designed to bear the weight of a single person, not an entire family. Get off your fatwagon and *do* something about it.

August 2013

The Duty of Intervention

• • •

Two RECENT PUBLIC DEATHS ARE weighing on my mind these days: Philip Seymour Hoffman's death from an apparent heroin overdose in apartment in New York City and, closer to home, the death by apparent exposure to the elements of a young man who was a senior at Denison University, the Ohio college I attended when I was his age and in whose precincts I now live, who had last been seen alive leaving a local bar at two in the morning.

Both these deaths are deeply tragic and worthy of more than private grief in that they cut short promising lives far before their time, and both were in a sense self-inflicted. But they also have in common a nagging question that affects us all but lingers unspoken after the horror and sadness sinks in: could these deaths have been avoided if the people in these men's lives had been more attentive or, having noticed something, if they had intervened? I don't mean the institutional responsibility of colleges, bar owners, or psychotherapists. I mean: what are the limits, within friendships and families, of intervention into the lives of those we love?

The inevitable public discourse about Hoffman's death has followed two themes: focus on the premature ending of a great acting career to the near-exclusion of any reflection or judgment on the cause of his death, as though he had been killed in a car crash or struck by lightning (Charlie Rose hosted two famous film critics in a half-hour discussion having just this tone). More recently there have been eloquent expressions by alcoholics and other substance abusers of the "there but for the grace of God" sort, their message being that no matter how clean you are or for how long, addiction never truly leaves your life and it is only by constant vigilance that the addict can hold it at bay.

Something is missing from this conversation. My first reaction upon hearing that Hoffman had been found with a needle in his arm and several dozen glassine envelopes of heroin in his apartment was not "what bad luck!" but "where were his friends and family?" How is it that a public man who must have interacted daily with dozens of people who presumably knew him well and cared for his well-being was able to conceal the lethal severity of his relapse into heroin addiction?

And if that relapse was detectable by at least some of those people, what on earth could have prevented them from doing something to intervene in a course of behavior that could kill him or, failing that, ruin his life? A perverted form of respect for individual choice? Fear of alienating a friend in whose fame they could bask? An overweening need to appear hip and non-judgmental about drug use?

These are not good answers, but they do raise the further question of what each of us would have done if we could, and what similar opportunities present themselves in our more quotidian lives when we suspect friends or family are at risk or in simple need. In the case of the local college student, he belonged to one of the most intimate college campuses in the country, whose main entrance was a block away from the bar he left in the middle of a frigid night. He was found several blocks in the opposite direction, face-down in the snow. Why was he leaving a bar alone at two a.m.? Why was no one with him? He was seen leaving; was he also seen to be drunk at the time, departing into one of the coldest winter nights in thirty years? Had he been depressed, worried, angry, giddy in the days before? Should someone have noticed any of these things and taken action?

I know nothing of these men's lives, really. Certainly not enough to judge whether anyone could have done anything differently. But you have to ask: are our communities too fragmented, our personal communications too centered on little screens to notice when a friend or relative or neighbor is in trouble? And if we do notice, do we err too much on the side of respecting others' privacy, their personal choices? Should someone have to ask for help before we are allowed to offer it or, much harder, to intrude into the situation?

No question: it's hard to intervene. That friend may not at all be issuing that cry for help that one remembers later, when it's too late. He may resist and evade and dissemble and deny, just as we might. He may call us rude for asking. But if we have been attentive, we may have noticed something that sets off an alarm in our heads. And the question is, what do we do then? Call the cops or his parents or his children? Convene a posse of close friends and confront him? Just follow him into that cold night? Or back off and hope for the best?

What does that person's trouble mean to us? Is it, as the coverage of the death of Philip Seymour Hoffman suggested, just one of those tragic things outside our control that happens every once in a sad while? Or is it our trouble too, and what's more, our obligation?

The stories of these unnecessary deaths should at least remind us that friendship – whether by blood or chance — is not just about participating in easy times, nor even about doing one's duty when it is obvious, nor, when all else has failed, coming together for funerals. It's about all that often unwelcome questioning and pushing and prodding and following in between.

February 2014

The Future of The Internet

• • •

YESTERDAY I WROTE AN EMAIL to a friend (using Gmail), and in it mentioned by name a hotel in Zihuatanejo, Mexico where my wife and I had stayed years ago. The hotel's name wasn't in the subject line; it was deep in the text of a rather lengthy email. That afternoon, while doing some online research on a magazine website, there appeared a banner ad for that same hotel. A bit later, I received an email (via Facebook) from one of the employees of that hotel, asking when we would be returning. Obviously none of this was coincidence: Google (or rather an algorithm created by Google) is reading my email, word for word, and selling information contained in it to third parties.

Despite the portrayal of the Internet as an agent of democratization and positive disruptive change (an image propagated mainly by self-aggrandizing entrepreneurs), it looks increasingly like a tool of vested commercial interests and governments, and we as users look increasingly like a bunch of sheep on our way to a fleecing (or worse). Market power is excessively concentrated in a few big corporate players who preemptively acquire every potential competitor, privacy is considered passé, data security is under constant siege, and the pervasive vacuity of social media — not to mention their susceptibility to manipulation and mob rule (witness Turkey turning Twitter off and on like a faucet, or the crowd-sourced kneecapping of Mozilla CEO Brendan Eich) – requires no further comment. Simply put, the Internet as we know it is an odd sort of technological monopoly that itself is begging for creative disruption.

Let's remember what "the Internet" is: a network of computer networks that began as a way for academics (mostly geeks at Stanford University) to communicate with each other and, not incidentally, with the Pentagon's Defense Advanced Research Projects Agency (DARPA), which funded the development of the hardware "backbone" of the nascent Internet. Starting in the '80s, private enterprise became increasingly involved in the expansion and integration of this backbone. Add hypertext (Stanford again), browsers and search engines, and you have the World Wide Web, which is what we used to call the largely commercially-driven Internet of today.

Today's Internet is a reincarnation of broadcast TV of the 1960s: an artificial monopoly producing "content" that is ostensibly offered for free, but is designed either to sell merchandise directly or to attract paid advertising. In the Sixties no one imagined paying money to receive TV on particular topics over a wire strung to your house, or from outer space via a satellite. It's not too far-fetched to imagine that smart money soon will turn to providing similarly diverse methods of computer networking — and not just new websites — to consumers.

The technical core of the Internet – and what makes it a de facto monopoly today — is not one operating system or brand of hardware, and certainly not the domain name address system run by ICANN, whose governance has recently been the subject of some hyperventilated editorials, but the TCP/IP data communication protocol – a set of arbitrary lines of computer code that define a network's architecture and act as a universal data traffic cop.

The TCP/IP protocol suite was developed by DARPA but later (in the 1990s) handed off to an international, non-governmental supervisory organization called the Internet Engineering Task Force. Adoption of the TCP/IP protocol as the foundation for what we now know as the Internet is pretty much a historical fluke. There were and are other such protocols out there, based on different networking priorities. Google is working on one designed to enhance transmission speeds, naturally called SPDY. The use of hypertext (without which we'd all be online illiterates) isn't dependent on a particular network protocol, just as there is more than one method of transmitting electricity through copper wires.

For the vast majority of us, the Internet has three primary functions: personal communication, which we desire to be truly private; shopping, which we desire to be truly secure; and research, which we desire to be accurate. Could these functions, among others, be delivered via a non-TCP/IP-based network, or via a range of alternative protocols, which might afford privacy, resistance to data trolling and targeted ads, truly secure data encryption, carefully curated content, or other desirable qualities currently missing from the Web, or which might simply be unique to a small, self-selected group of users?

Such "counter-internets" could be the future of the Internet. There might one day be as many Internets as there are channels on cable TV, each with a special purpose, user population, and attribute profile, and the capacity to circumvent the geopolitical and commercial balkanization that threatens the current model. However its future develops for better or worse, the monolithic Internet that we have today may not be as permanent as it looks.

April 2014

Is Our Entertainment Moral?

• • •

THIS MAY SEEM A STRANGE question, but it arises out of a recent experience that has set me thinking about some of our fundamental cultural assumptions.

My dear wife and I watched the Emmy awards show the other night, and learned with the rest of humanity that "Breaking Bad" won several honors, including Best Drama, and the other big winners and/or nominees were "True Detective" (about violent crime in the boondocks), "Scandal" (about political scandal), "House of Cards" (about a corrupt politician), "The Good Wife" (about a corrupt politician's wife), "Mad Men" (about adulterous and/or corrupt advertising executives), and "Game of Thrones" (about corrupt prehistoric politicians, internecine warfare, incest, and dragons).

More particularly (and of interest to me), the Outstanding Writing award nominees were the following: "Breaking Bad," "Game of Thrones," "House of Cards," and "True Detective."

Seeing that "Breaking Bad" won Best Drama over her beloved "Downton Abbey," my dear wife asked me what "Breaking Bad" was about, and I explained as best I could (having watched not a single episode in deference to her) that it was about a basically decent schoolteacher who is inexorably drawn into the seamy, violent world of dealing in illegal methamphetamines (forgive me if I got any of that wrong).

She then repeated a question that she had rather forcefully posed to me on one of our first dates over a decade ago (when I had foolishly taken her to see the film "Collateral," in which, as you may recall, Tom Cruise plays a mob assassin who forces an innocent cab driver to drive him around while he knocks people off): why would anyone want to watch such a thing? Why deliberately (and at the cost of real money) expose oneself to graphic violence, betrayal, shame, crime — the very worst of human behavior and experience – for *entertainment*?

The question can easily be dismissed as amusingly naïve or closed-minded; indeed, what may be most interesting about the question is not any particular answer to it but the reflexive certainty with which we judge it to be a silly question. Yet I've learned to take my wife's questions seriously, and I therefore proceeded in my bumbling way to defend modern entertainment in general and the world of TV and movies in particular. I utterly failed to persuade her, which is not surprising; but more interestingly, I also failed to convince myself. Let me try again.

One of my dear wife's other favorite questions about movies, usually asked during the opening credits, is "Is this true?" By this she means: "Is what I'm about to see a true story, or has someone made it up?" If the answer is the latter, she is immediately skeptical to the point of outright resistance; if the former, she is cautiously receptive. (We watch a lot of documentaries.)

So in part the question of the morality of modern entertainment has to do with the virtue (if any) of fictional narrative itself, which (as I pointed out on the night of the Emmys) is as old as man. Why do we tell made-up stories to one another, and are those reasons good or bad ones?

At the virtuous end of the spectrum must be *empathy*: the creation and experience of fictional narrative forces us to see the world through the eyes of others; it broadens our experience beyond what a single life could encompass; it defeats the human limitations of time and place and makes us more communal beings. The experience of empathy is surely a good thing, though it must be said that purely factual narrative – some kinds of journalism – could provide the same. What is it about *fiction* that is virtuous or moral?

Fiction in its creation is a craft like any other – seizing common elements and shaping them into something that may not have existed previously in the world, and might never exist without the artist's intervention. There are many chairs in the world, but none of them quite like the chair I might make in my garage (were I so foolish as to attempt such a thing). It has the stamp of me on it, my preference in woods, my competence or lack thereof with a lathe. Of course much fiction is autobiographical, utterly imitative of the real world, but it still has the stamp of a particular sensibility on it, because those are the rules of fiction: the author gets to choose how the heroine looks, what she says, because the author wants to communicate something that mere facts might not make so clear.

The audience's experience of fictional narrative is fraught with the awareness that craft is afoot, that *choices have been made*, and that those choices are not necessarily bound by reality or experience. Much of our judging of the quality of fictional narrative is an evaluation of those choices, as well as of the execution of the craft. Our curiosity about those choices and the quality of that execution is what draws us toward the primordial campfire around which made-up stories are continually being told. We don't know what will happen, because anything can. The author plays God, and we practice being in the hands of God.

I'd argue that that uncertainty about what will happen in a story is a virtuous experience, one in which it is good to be habituated. We all could use a bit less certainty in our opinions and prejudices and expectations of the world, and I think narrative fiction instills that openness.

But we haven't yet addressed what my dear wife is really objecting to when "Breaking Bad" trounces "Downton Abbey" at the Emmys. Even if we grant that fictional narrative has, at least potentially, inherent virtue, what makes the story of a drug dealer or a murderer or a serial adulterer or an evil sorceress worth watching – indeed, *more* worth watching than the story of some over-dressed, deluded, but mostly harmless aristocrats in a big house in England? To put my wife's thesis plainly: watching violence makes us more violent; watching corruption corrupts absolutely. This may not be provable with scientific certainty, but nor can we disprove it. Granting that we would all defend to the death one another's right to consume the dark matter on our screens, the question remains: why do it?

Evidently we like it. The anti-heroes of last century's literature and "The Sopranos" may have started us down this path, but the current cultural preference for shock and shame, for "Breaking Bad" over "Downton Abbey," seems in part a juvenile response to the increase in sheer permissiveness afforded by the advent of cable, just as surely as advancements in computer-generated graphics made a "Transformers" movie franchise all but inevitable. We show it because we can. The merely possible can crowd out the good, and sometimes we overgrown children want to see the possible just for the sheer spectacle of it. (I myself will confess to sheer glee at seeing the Marvel comic book heroes of my youth brought to life on the big screen by middle-aged filmmakers who, like me, grew up with them and take them somewhat seriously.)

The immorality of narrative fiction – not limited to movies and TV – is of course most evident when its primary effect is titillation. When we're just watching for the sex scenes or the shot of someone's boobs or the gore of a horrible death, then we're debased in the way that my wife fears. Most of us can recognize –and have experienced – fiction that calls mainly on our most reptilian sensibilities, that merely exploits our prurient fascination with sex, gore, and evil, that parades human frailty mainly to mock it or to allow us to feel superior. There is certainly much junk being made, and a great deal of it is on cable and in the movie theaters. Expensive, well-made, well-marketed, lucrative junk. And my dear wife is right to question why we watch it, or read it, for surely too many of us do, and in so doing insure that there will be much more of it.

Violence and sex and human evil are all part of the artist's toolbox no matter the medium, because they are part of life; they can make a story more believable, or delineate what to avoid, or reconnect us to sensual pleasure, or allow the story to convey an otherwise unbelievable truth. As I say, I haven't seen a single episode of "Breaking Bad," but I'm prepared to believe that its virtues are as old as stagecraft: illustration of the frailty of human life, instruction in the ambiguity of human action and the unpredictability of its consequences, reminders of the potential for cruelty and dishonesty and occasional redemption and forgiveness in all of us; all of the grim particulars of the protagonists' experience, made ours.

Then there's the wonder of good acting, the sheer amazement at watching someone transform himself with complete authenticity into someone completely different. This adds another layer to the awareness of craft that distinguishes narrative fiction from the rest of our experience.

Who is to say when craft is misemployed, when it's been applied to the wrong ends? Only each of us, and we're lucky that it's still our choice. My wife has clearly made hers.

I'm still not sure I answered her question.

August 2014

Illiberal Arts:
Does College Have a Future?

• • •

OCCASIONALLY - NOT OFTEN - A MAINSTREAM print magazine publishes a piece that actually does what long-form journalism is supposed to do: make you stop and reassess a personal belief.

One of mine is in the value of a liberal arts education like the one I received, which launched me on a largely happy and hugely lucky life, and which serves me to this day. But in the *New Yorker* last week appeared a "Letter from Oberlin: The Big Uneasy," wherein the author, Nathan Heller, interviews a number of students and faculty members at small, elite Oberlin College in Ohio and describes the students' utter dissatisfaction with their college experiences. And while it's unlikely that the attitudes captured in the article are representative of today's college students, much of it calls into question the very viability of the small, private liberal arts college.

Oberlin has always been a famously left-leaning place, and the students interviewed for the article are the sort who can spout lines like "…this institution functions on the premises of imperialism, white supremacy, capitalism, ableism, and cissexist heteropatriarchy," which reads like satire of leftist vocabulary *du jour*. (I infer that "ableism" must be the prejudice that the able unavoidably bear toward the disabled, but I can't be sure. Other neologisms mentioned in the article include "allyship" (as contrasted with "collaboration," which is insufficiently deferential to the oppressed), "intersectionality" (alluding, I gather, to the grid of vectors of racial or sexual bias), and of course "cisgender" (almost mainstream now, meaning birth gender, to allow for the possibility that you may have discarded yours). My personal favorite, though, is "microaggressions," which I visualize as a horde of nanobots scurrying about inflicting tiny injuries, like mosquitoes. My childhood, I now realize, was basically composed of microaggressions. But on college campuses today, they are the sinister background hum of societal injustice, to be called out and eradicated.)

The semi-radicalized minority and/or economically underprivileged students interviewed in the article (who would probably find being so labelled a microaggression at the very least) are easy to dismiss as oversensitive, spoiled, ungrateful, and fatally naïve (not to mention hypocritical, as why would one remain for even one semester in the thrall of an imperialist heteropatriarchy that one is free to leave?). One of them complains that his being allowed to show his understanding of course material by simply chatting with his professor for a while, rather than taking a written exam like the rest of his classmates, isn't "institutionalized." "I have to *find* that professor," he moans, as though the exception being made for him is cruelly insufficient. One wonders what becomes of such a person in the real working world, where the nuances of identity politics are reduced to "who is my boss?"

Of course, college has always been a hiatus from the real world, a place where young people are sent to extend their adolescence and act out its privileges of idealism and self-indulgence. I came of college age in the late Sixties, and attended another small liberal arts school in Ohio, Denison University. It was and is more conservative and less selective than Oberlin, but it was and is otherwise quite similar: a small, private, coed liberal arts college in the rural Midwest whose applicants were mostly white and well-off and drawn from suburban environments. When I was enrolled, there were perhaps a dozen black students, and a handful of Asians. The LGBT rights movement was not yet on the horizon. Denison today is, thankfully, a dramatically more diverse place.

Even as a white kid from the suburbs, my own college experience ran the gamut from difficult to trying. The nineteen-sixties were, if anything, even more culturally turbulent than today: the twin causes of civil rights (by which was meant equal rights for black people) and the opposition to the war in Vietnam (and to the military draft, which actually touched each of us, unlike the wars of today) thoroughly permeated our college experiences, permanently radicalizing some of us, making lifelong liberals of others, and hardening the conservatism of still others. My generation's brand of activism was no less confrontational than that of today's disaffected students: minority groups submitted "nonnegotiable demands" to college presidents, marches and sit-ins were common, classes were routinely suspended, administration buildings occupied and, famously, students shot dead in the midst of an anti-war protest at Kent State. Oberlin and Denison today seem rather mild by comparison.

Then as now, a basic liberal principle at work in the admissions policies of most private liberal arts colleges was that cultural/racial/economic/sexual diversity on a college campus benefits not only the minorities who are thus included, but the non-minority students (white, middle- or upper-class heterosexuals) who are thus allowed –or forced—to associate with those minorities. Diversity is, in this world view, inherently good. What could go wrong?

But Heller's piece articulates a contradiction at the heart of this liberal notion:

> *"Today, [these minorities] are told that they belong [at an elite college], but they also must take on an extracurricular responsibility: doing the work of diversity. They move their lives to rural Ohio and perform their identities, whatever that might mean. They bear out the school's vision. In exchange, they're groomed for old-school entry into the liberal upper middle class. An irony surrounds the whole endeavor, and a lot of students seemed to see it."*

The transaction described here –come and give us your unique, individual traits (unspoken: "which are the product of some form of adversity or deprivation") and we'll give you the keys to a "better" life as generations of predominantly white, Western, middle-class heterosexuals have defined and lived it – is at minimum a deeply patronizing bargain, and it raises questions about what "affirmative action" is really all about: redressing old exclusionary wrongs, certainly, but also commodifying diversity, turning it into another aspect of a curriculum, another campus perk, to be consumed by the mostly white, well-off students whose parents are willing and able to pay for it.

None of this is evil, and some of it, thankfully, is compelled by law. But it does imply a conflict of interest on the part of institutions that seek to attract minority and underprivileged students, and raises the question whether those students are being well-served by the colleges they've been recruited to enhance. It seems entirely plausible that the benefits of diversity are, as often as not, a one-way street, and that the students who complain in the report from Oberlin about being conned and deeply wronged by their college should be taken at their word, and should have been encouraged to go elsewhere, not because they weren't wanted or couldn't succeed, but because to admit them was in some ways exploitative.

And that raises another question: from these students' perspective, what is the purpose of a liberal arts education in the first place? What would the college they wish they were enrolled in look like, if not like elitist, privileged Oberlin?

As a crudely practical matter, a liberal arts education is about becoming certified as having completed it. It is an extended tribal membership ritual, and the tribe being auditioned for is, by definition, the society of people who have been similarly educated. If that's not for you, either because you have better things to do with your time or your goal is membership in an entirely different tribe, then better to just say no to it.

Like most forms of education, the secularly ecumenical higher education offered by the typical liberal arts college is both programmatic (a prescribed body of knowledge is taught) and standards-based (you'll be judged by how well you've learned it). There are many other premises essential to higher education, but without these two, you have something other than a college, and something short of a reason to go there, no matter how many trigger warnings you receive or how many safe spaces you are promised.

Yet it's clear that these are exactly the aspects of their college experience that the Oberlin students interviewed most dislike: they are made to follow a curriculum devised by people unlike (meaning, among other things, better educated than) themselves, and they are judged by their proficiency in mastering that curriculum. They also don't like the fact that the resulting job of education conflicts with the job of activism (a difficult balancing of two desirable goals reminiscent of, say, being a working mother), and that, in being exposed to an intellectual environment, they are sometimes challenged in ways they find disturbing to their sense of emotional safety, justice, or right-thinking. In response, they systematically suppress, marginalize, or run from ideas and voices that don't correspond to their own. Guest speakers of undeniable worldly stature are shouted down or dis-invited because they represent insufficiently enlightened views; conservative professors must keep their opinions in the closet. As one professor put it, "my leftist students are doing the right wing's job for it." By which she means: the standards of liberal education –of which the free exchange of ideas is perhaps the most sacred — are being trampled by liberals.

If there can be no agreement about standards – both that they are necessary and what they should measure — there is really no space for education to happen. This is as true of purely "vocational" training (and what education isn't that?) as it is of the more ethereal subjects on offer at a liberal arts college. The rub is that standards are inherently hierarchical, judgmental, and meritocratic, and we should frankly acknowledge that not everyone belongs in a social system (like a college, or a corporation, or a law firm, hospital, or military corps) that operates on those principles.

The Oberlin piece made me once again wonder about the future of the private liberal arts college. If the experience and attitudes of the Oberlin students interviewed are not unusual, their college and mine are living on borrowed time, merely postponing a well-deserved obsolescence, their academic and admissions standards not only compromised and culturally conflicted but, more importantly, ill-suited to prepare their post-millennial graduates for the tectonic shifts in labor markets and cultural norms that will define their adult lives.

Small liberal arts colleges are in many ways sized for failure: not big enough to attract and accommodate diversity in a natural, organic way or to benefit from economies of scale, but too big to change course quickly or avoid being hamstrung by their clashing constituencies. The better models, particularly for minorities, but ultimately for most students, may be either much larger places – the great private and state universities, where true diversity is built in by sheer numbers and huge endowments – or much smaller and more individualized venues, like online curricula, or college-level versions of charter schools, where localized interests can be directly addressed and idiosyncratic sensitivities can be genuinely accommodated without tossing standards overboard.

Ironically, liberal arts colleges risk becoming the walking dead of higher education not because they have failed to live up to the liberal ideal of diversity, but because they have become so beholden to it that their first principles are compromised. An institution that can even contemplate acceding to student demands for emotional safety and social comfort at the expense of free speech and intellectual rigor has outlived its usefulness as a place of higher learning and should perhaps consider becoming, more openly, a theme park.

If only for demographic reasons, the days are rapidly waning when a liberal arts college can survive by subsidizing diversity with the tuition and alumni contributions of a shrinking white, straight majority, while accommodating illiberal behavior and lax standards in the name of that diversity. The marketplace will ultimately render a harsh judgment of such places and their graduates. A new paradigm, just as inclusive but more engaged with the world, more truly liberal –and therefore much less sheltered and sheltering — needs to emerge with intra-generational speed.

June 2016

Orlando

• • •

OK, LET'S THINK ABOUT THIS.

Guy goes into a gay nightclub at two in the morning, the tail of a Saturday night, and shoots people. Dozens die. They get the exact number wrong. Most people killed in a "mass shooting" in U.S. history. A record of some kind. The guy is a citizen, U.S.-born, but has proclaimed his ties to Al Qaeda and, just before he is put down by a SWAT team, to ISIS.

First thought: guns. Prevent people from having assault rifles and maybe this won't happen, or won't happen as often. But we know where that thought goes. It goes up against the *Heller* decision, Scalia reaching out from his grave, and the NRA, and every self-imagined revolutionary cowboy out there, and it's not as though this isn't just a lens collecting in one place a few of the hundreds of deaths-by-gun happening every week in U.S. cities. And the wind goes out of it and the thought dies. These people are determined, we're told. If we take their guns away, they'll just build bombs out of pressure cookers or load trucks with explosives. Myself, I guess I'd like to make them jump through those extra hoops, test that determination a bit. Just a thought.

Second thought: politics. More xenophobic fodder for Trump, more ineffectual gesturing from Obama, more talk of terrorism as though this guy was anything but another narcissist moron with a gun looking for a justification for his pathology, what we used to call simply a murderer without the need to elevate him into an enemy combatant. It's like calling a thief a soldier. More talk from Rubio about how it's not the weapon but the ideology that we must somehow control, as though you can shame an ideology with the phrase "Islamic terrorism" or control it with –what? More guns? And of course the FBI interviewed the guy in 2013 after he mouthed off at work about Al Qaeda. This catch-and-release trope is getting overly familiar. Has anyone thought about the possibly radicalizing effect of being interrogated by the FBI?

Third thought: media. More grist for the media mills, sending their reporters to Orlando to stand in the street where it happened, an odd throwback to old TV, as though personal presence has any meaning anymore, unless you're there, actually there, when it happens, and get a video of it on your phone. Ratings bumps, a couple of news cycles on this, at least. (If we can't bring ourselves to enact serious gun control, let's enact a Murderer Effacement Act, which would make it a federal crime to publish the name or the likeness or any personal details about anyone committing a mass shooting. Would present First Amendment issues, but by now should pass the yelling-fire-in-a-crowded-theater test.) More talk about the true Islam and community involvement. Sanctimony about the gay angle, punditry about hate crime and solidarity with our gay friends, moments of silence, ritual flower altars in the street next to the club. Seen it all before, it's losing its capacity to horrify or titillate or inspire; a couple of news cycles on this, at most.

Not many thoughts. Then acceptance, silence, receptivity before the screens. A hundred more angry young men notice the attention being paid, want it for themselves. Next time. Soon.

June 2016

How to Prevent the Next Lone Wolf

• • •

Much of the media coverage of the Orlando massacre has focused on the shooter, a young-ish Muslim man, who shall remain, at least here, nameless. His father, his ex-wife and wife (now widow) have been interviewed, his family and work history excavated, his psychological profile pontificated upon, his selfies spread across the Internet and on the front pages of national newspapers, his claim of allegiance to ISIS seized upon, analyzed, and bandied about for political purposes, his name repeated endlessly, all with the ostensible purpose of somehow understanding what caused him to enter a gay nightclub and gun down dozens of people with a semi-automatic weapon. Who *was* this guy, and what motivated him? Was it hate, was it terrorism, was it madness? We need to know.

The only high-minded argument for this kind of scrutiny of a massmurderer is that, in understanding him, we will be able to prevent this sort of thing from happening in the future; authorities will be better able to profile and interdict future perpetrators, and we will be enabled to detect them in our communities. But there is of course little evidence of this; vigilance over one's neighbors curdles quickly into bigotry, and the frequency of mass murder in the US has increased rather than diminished in this age of 24/7 news cycles and perpetually talking heads –psychiatrists, security experts, former police chiefs — who all too willingly offer their expertise to the maw of media commerce. No, the attention paid to individuals responsible for atrocities like this stems from baser impulses, ones that we would do well to resist.

In an era when the only qualification of a presumptive nominee for the presidency is his celebrity, it's no surprise that we tend to focus on personal identity when we seek explanations for the inexplicable. In the grip of outrage, we have a childlike wish for a story, for a neat linear narrative we can follow like our favorite TV drama. News organizations are now barefacedly in the business of entertainment, and we are addicted to the transient titillations they offer. Their focus on the person of the shooter is less about prevention than it is about their product and our prurience. Hence news anchors are shipped to Orlando to stand pointlessly in the street near the site of the crime, and we linger voyeuristically on the words of the survivors. This is exploitation, not news, and certainly not an exercise in prevention.

Even the language of the current examination is shaped into the tropes of drama. To call what played out in that nightclub a "tragedy" is to misunderstand both the origins of that word and the event. It was a heinous crime willfully perpetrated by a single man, and nothing like the true tragedies of disease, natural disaster, accident or botched intention that tear at our hearts because they arise not out of madness or evil, but out of fatal chance or simple human frailty.

We respond to tragedy with empathic sadness. And certainly we empathize with those who lost loved ones in that nightclub, those who still suffer their wounds. But the man who caused this? Our response to him should be a cold indifference to who he was, how he came to be, and what he intended, for we already know the answers, time and experience and common sense have taught us those answers, and he can teach us nothing. He is undeserving of our attention, and to turn it on him only serves his perverted purposes and, worse, ensures that there will be more like him.

This is not to suggest that we ignore the crime, or the ongoing risk of home-grown terrorism. Independent of the public fixation on the shooter and his motivations, there is a real investigation going on, conducted by professionals whose working lives are devoted to understanding, preventing, and punishing crimes like this. We should support and applaud them, and help them to go about their work, but otherwise ignore the criminal.

"We have a right to know!" cry the media drones whose jobs depend on this sort of endless, pointless, unilluminating attention to a personage deserving of none of it. But when does our wish to know, our addiction to dramatic narrative, collide with our self-interest? Though there is no evidence that the sort of attention being devoted to the Orlando shooter will reduce the likelihood of another event like this, there is every reason to believe that the posthumous fame and political dignification of this criminal as an ideological terrorist will incite more imitators, more young, deluded, angry, pathological aspirants to the media validation they see him receiving. If prevention of lone wolf attacks is a percentage game, we are worsening our chances by advertising a model for the hundred or thousand undecided thugs out there, hunched over their smartphones and dreaming of the fame we will heap on them when they, too, abandon hope and decency.

What if our cultural norm, rather than to reward mass murderers with unremitting attention, was to consign them to the oblivion they rightly deserve, to erase them from cultural memory rather than brand them into it? There is a template for this in Japan, where violent crime is rarely reported because it is rare, and rare in part because it is rarely reported, as if to underscore the societal shame it engenders.

If he were convinced that no attention would be paid to him or his family or his supposed cause, would the next psychopath be as inclined to plan the next bloodbath? What if there were a federal law – call it the Mass Murderer Effacement Act of 2016 – that prohibited the publication of the name, likeness, or personal details about anyone committing multiple murder? Leave aside whether such a law could pass Constitutional muster (arguably it could, as what more "compelling state interest" would one need than the prevention of another Orlando?); would we really lose anything of value in our awareness and understanding of current events? Would our freedom of speech be infringed in any way that matters in real life?

The current media frenzy over the Orlando shooter is like pouring nutrients on a lethal bacterium and hoping it will die. We need to cultivate a judgmental indifference to the personal narrative of evil, and suppress our fascination with it. The only rewards for perpetrators of mass violence should be silence, dismissal, and quick justice.

June 2016

Meditations

· · ·

ANNIVERSARY
(On the 10th anniversary of my mother's death)

If I could crack open your heart
unstick the clotted care and make it flow again
undo my failures, or do the penance they deserve
I could save myself and you
be the superman I wanted to be
as a child in my underwear, towel tied round my neck
jumping from the sofa.

There is no redemption that fits this.
God forgives, I see that every sundown
but you are made of sterner stuff
like the dreams from which I wake groggy with loss:
we're always traveling, always late for somewhere, something.
I am always unready, taken by surprise.

If I could smooth that brow with fingers that would make it stay
I would keep it secret
I would wait until the time was right
the next breath, for instance.
My next stop would be the hospital
to perform other miracles, towel flying behind me.
I'd hide behind doors and cheer children
steal worry away from old women
silence crying
replace it with a lifting sigh
that would color the night.

I would then use my power
to travel back in time
ten years
and tell you what I'd done
to see your pride one last time.
You'd frown at the towel, but I'd bargain with you awhile
For more time, and other powers
things you might grant me now
but could not then.

October 2013

The Lesson of the Two Shoes

• • •

You walk through life, aware of what you are aware of. How much are we missing? I was recently reminded to ask this of myself more frequently. It was a lesson of two shoes.

I was in Washington, D.C. for a business meeting. I'd flown in the night before and stayed in a hotel within walking distance of the meeting venue. In the morning, I rose and showered and shaved and put on the suit and tie that I'd brought for the occasion. Finally I put on my dress shoes and headed out the door.

It was a beautiful spring morning and the walk to the meeting was only a few blocks. I passed dozens of other people on their way to work. Midway to my destination, I noticed that one shoe was chafing the sides of my foot. I laughed to myself, realizing that I get dressed up so infrequently these days that my feet had expanded in response to going barefoot most of the time. But why did only one foot hurt?

I hurried on to the designated office building and spent the morning at a large conference table surrounded by other carefully-dressed men and women. Around lunch time, thoroughly bored, I glanced down under the table and saw, to my horror, that on one foot I wore one of my nicest dress shoes, and the other foot bore one-half of the pair casual shoes I'd worn down on the plane the day before. They weren't even remotely similar to one another.

I kept my feet well under the table for the remainder of the meeting, and positively scurried to the bathroom and back when I eventually had to go. Later I made a similarly furtive dash back to my hotel and across the huge lobby, thronging with other guests who I was sure were hugely amused by my ingenuity in footwear.

How had this happened, for the first time in thousands of mornings of getting dressed for work? Yes, I was in an unfamiliar place and had gotten dressed in the early morning gloom of my room. Yes, I was less accustomed to getting dressed in a hurry than I once was, back when my life included dressing for office work on a daily basis. But really; not to notice that I was putting on two different shoes, and to continue to miss this fact as I proceeded to walk ten blocks in broad daylight across busy city streets? My eyesight was perfect, so that couldn't be the excuse. Had I really become so oblivious? Was this some precursor of early-onset dementia?

Ironically, part of the problem may have been my recently-enhanced vision, bestowed by my ophthalmologist in the form of a perfectly focused new synthetic lens in each eye. I was still wandering through the world in subdued awe, gazing intently at distant sights where I once might have been merely staring at my shoes. This was a good thing.

But still: I had been oblivious to something that should have been obvious, simply because I was on autopilot, overly focused on a narrow, immediate goal.

A lesson, then: never, never assume that you're seeing the whole picture. There may be a detail, just beyond the periphery of your vision, that could change everything. In focusing several steps ahead, you may be neglecting something near at hand that is critical to the process. Look around the corner, or under the table; do the occasional mental 360.

Another, larger lesson: be skeptical of what you think you're aware of, especially when that awareness conforms to your expectations or reinforces your belief in your own correctness. It's often when we're the most confident that we're the most wrong.

Finally: when your feet hurt, pay attention.

October 2013

The Parable of the Asian Ladybug

• • •

It's late October in Ohio, and the ladybugs are swarming.

Not the bright red ladybugs of childhood and picture-books, but the "multicolored Asian lady beetle," as they are formally called (*Harmonia axyridis*, for you taxonomy and/or Latin fans). They have the familiar beetle-backed shape so lovingly stolen by Volkswagen designers those many years ago, but are dirty brown in color, sometimes with the ladybug's traditional black spots, sometimes not. They fly in that awkward, slow, ladybug way of flying, barely achieving liftoff, wings sprouting from under half-shells of carapace, and they're on everything right now – in your clothing and hair after you cross the yard, in the trees, all over the outside of your house, and some make their way into the interiors, crawling up drapes and across floors, where they make an unsettling crunching sound if you happen to step on them.

Which you evidently should try not to do, for at least two reasons, neither of them spiritual: first, their blood, when spilled, stains permanently and stinks to high heaven (evidently the best evolution could do for them as a defense mechanism was regret –- as in "you can kill me, but you'll regret it"). Secondly, they are helpful predators, eating mostly things with which we have less sentimental attachment than them, such as aphids and other pests we would otherwise kill with chemicals.

They're called Asian because we imported them from Asia in a number of "planned releases" by the U.S. Department of Agriculture, embarked upon in an effort to control indigenous insect tree pests. (Yes, yet another example of Federal government overreach, though as this occurred mostly in the 1970's and '80's, this one can't be blamed on Obama.) This "worked" in a sense (pecan crops have benefitted enormously), but like so many other species that are brought here, deliberately or otherwise, from other lands (the voracious Asian killer carp currently colonizing the Great Lakes springs to mind), the Asian ladybugs do so well here that they've outnumbered the local variety and proliferated to the point of -shall we say- diminishing returns.

Evidently they swarm your house because they believe they're still in outer Mongolia and perceive your house as a cliff-face where they can cozy up and spend the winter. Many of them have succeeded in wintering inside our house, I can tell you that. And biking or running on our neighborhood bike path has become a determinedly close-mouthed exercise.

Still, small price to pay, right? They only become a total nuisance right around Halloween, in which respect they are certainly not alone.

I caught one today, ambling up our bedroom curtain in search of a really nice place to spend the winter. I caught it easily and cupped it in my palm, briefly considering flushing it down the toilet. But then a thought struck me: is this how God thinks of *us*? Basically a nuisance, but a nuisance of his own creation, one that started with the best of intentions, not likely to survive very long, easily destroyed, but occasionally, sometimes, maybe even most of the time, still doing some small bit of good?

I walked all the way downstairs, opened the back door, opened my hand, and watched it fly slowly, awkwardly away.

October 2013

11/22/63

• • •

ONE OF THE PRIVILEGES OF living as long as some of us have is that you get to witness a respectable amount of history. I have clear personal memories of Bill Mazeroski's walk-off home run to win the 1960 World Series for Pittsburgh, Alan Shepard's ride into space in 1962, John Glenn's orbiting of the earth a year later, the Beatles' appearance on that famous Ed Sullivan Show in 1964, the shootings of Martin Luther King and Bobby Kennedy in 1968, the long string of Gemini and Apollo missions leading up to the moon landing in 1969, the War in Vietnam, which we called simply the War, and which distorted my college years with the threat of being drafted, the resignation of Richard Nixon from the presidency in 1974 in the wake of Watergate, the killing of John Lennon in the lobby of his New York apartment building in 1980. You can divide humanity between those who have a living memory of these things and those who will only read about them, should they even care to.

But looming above all these events for those of us who lived through them is one harrowing moment that changed life in America and how we conceived of it, forever. That was when, 50 years ago, the President of the United States was assassinated. It was the 9/11 of my generation, in that nothing that ever followed would seem quite as inconceivable.

I was a kid in junior high school in a suburb of Pittsburgh, and boys in those days lived for space. I mean outer space, as we called it then, and it was a glorious time to be alive and young if you cared about science, or what we understood to be science, as I deeply did then, and about the prospect of space travel, which we assumed would become commonplace in our lifetimes.

Imagine being a boy like that in the greatest country in the world, and that country declares that its top priority is to put a man on the moon within a handful of years. Even a kid can be patient for that long.

And the man who declared this was younger than my father, and handsome, and had, like my father, a beautiful wife, and didn't wear a hat like most men did then, and didn't even wear an overcoat on cold days, didn't seem to need it or to care, and had a habit of running his hand through his thick hair, and hung out with his brother, and was President of the United States. I didn't know anything about politics, but I liked him.

On the day he was shot we were in school, as it was a Friday. We were asked to return to what we called our home rooms, which was unusual at that time of the day, nearing mid-afternoon, almost time to go home, the yellow buses lined up in the circle outside the school, and I went as told, like everyone else, to my home room. And there was a TV in the room, another anomaly, wheeled in on a metal cart and plugged into the wall, and then Walter Cronkite was on the screen saying that the President had been shot in Dallas and then, a little later, that the President was dead.

What I mainly remember of that moment was looking out at the buses lined up outside, the late autumn light slanting through the windows of our classroom, and thinking that my parents' world had changed, and that therefore my world had changed, and I didn't know how. Everything seemed as orderly as before, everything seemed to be under control, but what we had just been told suggested that all that was a pleasant lie.

We had the weekend to begin to mourn and watch TV, which was given over entirely to the event. There were no commercials, no programming, nothing but the continual reporting of what had happened and what would happen next. My mother, married to a Republican, admitted tearfully to my father that she had voted for Kennedy, which shocked and angered him, as it meant that his vote, three years before, had been neutralized. My younger brother and I looked on in awe.

On Sunday, incredibly, there was another public shooting, as the man who had been arrested for killing the President was shot in turn by another man, this time on television. Clearly the world had come loose from its moorings; the violence of fiction and movies had invaded the real world, never to retreat. That same day Kennedy's casket was moved on a caisson (a word we learned that day) along Pennsylvania Avenue, led by a riderless black horse, high empty boots backwards in the stirrups, symbolism from a bygone age, yet immediately understood.

Kennedy was buried on Monday, a national day of mourning. Schools were closed and we again watched TV all day, watched the dead President's three-year old son improbably, heartbreakingly, salute his father's casket as it passed by (I try to imagine my grandson, three years old this month, doing this and cannot), watched the woman we knew even then as Jackie with her black veil floating in the wind at Arlington, a place I didn't then know but would come to, as she and her husband's brother lit a flame at the President's grave, and declared it eternal.

On Tuesday we went back to school. There was little talk about "closure" in those days; I don't think the term had yet been invented. There was certainly less belief in the need for kids our age to express our anxieties. The instinct of our teachers was exactly the opposite: get back to business, make them work, take them out of themselves and back into the worlds of Latin and chemistry and *Moby-Dick*. And so we did what we were told.

But we were anxious, and the world had changed, and would never be quite right again. In a very few years Martin Luther King would be shot and then, a mere two months later, Bobby Kennedy too, the completion of an awful triptych of murders of public men that seemed, by then, almost inevitable. I remember being awakened by my mother on the morning after Bobby Kennedy's assassination (we were still in Pittsburgh, too many time zones from L.A. to have learned at the moment it occurred) and, when she told me the news, lying in my bed thinking, first, "Oh no," and then, "Of course."

On the summer night a year later while I waited, rapt, in the rec room of my girlfriend's home for Armstrong to climb down onto the face of the moon, I thought back, as we all did, to Kennedy and his resolution that this night would come. And come it had, in part as a tribute to what we had lost, and were still losing. After a few more trips, we stopped going to the moon, and it became clear that my childhood dreams of living in outer space were just that.

By the day John Lennon was killed I was so completely an adult that I was getting divorced. I lived in New York then, as he had, and I and my wife up to that day ignored our lawyers and fell to comforting each other over the papers that would send us on our separate trajectories, in fresh disbelief that even our music could be taken from us by yet another fool with a gun.

The cliché is that we lost our innocence that day in Dallas, but that doesn't quite capture what had happened. We were never innocent, and we weren't so lost that we wouldn't still get to the moon. But we had believed in a fundamental civility to American public life, to the life of adults, a world of order that had been built up from our infancy in a million small expectations met and niceties observed and rules enforced. That web of order is what Oswald's bullets tore away from us. It was in a horrible way a liberation; we were thereafter able more easily to become the rebellious, wastrel generation we became, to stand up to our parents, to reject the War, to embrace that loss of civility as a sign of freedom. And eventually, as the songs predicted and as we knew in our hearts, we were to take over the broken world that day bequeathed to us.

So when September 11, 2001 came 'round to claim us, we of my generation were in a sorry way prepared.

November 2013

Last Chance Lost: Remembering Joel

• • •

DEATH MEANS MANY THINGS, BUT one thing it means is that our chances are finite.

The other day I learned that a friend and mentor of my youth, Joel P. Smith, had died at the age of 80. It is not too much to say that there was a time in my life when I idolized this man, in some ways still do, nor is it too much to say that my knowing him –his influence on me, the bits of his world that he shared with me — changed my life, made me a fundamentally different person than I would have been otherwise.

To which one might say: so what? It's the story of uncounted callow youths and their more worldly mentors since time began, and the changes wrought in me by my knowing him matter mainly to me alone. But in its particulars, and by way of honoring a lost friend, it's a story worth retelling.

I met Joel in 1970, when he was president of Denison University and I was an undergraduate senior there. He was 36 years old at the time, which is to say, among other things, that he was an extraordinarily young college president in an extraordinarily tumultuous time. The war in Vietnam — one of the most divisive wars in our nation's history– was raging, universal military conscription — which we called simply "the draft" — was a major and potentially lethal stumbling block in the life of every young male, and the country was in the throes of countercultural and civil rights movements that would, in fact, change the world. College campuses had become the epicenters of these upheavals, and Denison was no exception. There were sit-ins and be-ins and teach-ins, arguments across the political divide around every dining hall table, marches and demonstrations, speeches and shouting matches. Almost all of it was peaceful, but that doesn't mean it was always temperate or even civil.

Joel Smith's problem was that while he was a social liberal, he was at heart a conservative when it came to educational philosophy and how "the life of the mind" - a favorite phrase of his - should be conducted at a place like a private college. Formerly Dean of Students and Provost at Stanford University, a boy from a small town in Wisconsin who had transformed himself by sheer innate intelligence and hard work into a Marshall Scholar, then a lawyer, then an academician, he was above all a determined believer in "standards," a word he used often but which, in the world of the 1970s, had become synonymous with "elitist," as close to an obscenity as one needed back then. On campus he was regularly called that and much worse.

It didn't help him that he was so young, and so good-looking. What male faculty member could tolerate a guy who could not only match wits and academic pedigrees with you, and argue you into a corner, but also looked like a cross between Clint Eastwood (as he looked then) and George Clooney (as he would look thirty years later)? It was entirely too much. Joel was a lightning rod for the roiling emotions and opinions that gripped the campus in that fractious time.

I too was all about standards; having learned how to at least appear to meet them during my time at Denison, they were my protection and my pathway. I was about to graduate and was trying to decide, if I could avoid being sent to Vietnam, whether I would go to law school or, as my English professors would have preferred, pursue an advanced degree in English literature at one of the institutions where they had supported me for fellowships and stipends.

Joel somehow heard about me; I suppose I was, in his mind, what Denison was supposed to be about: a certain kind of self-realization that would either blossom in the real world or be crushed by it. He invited me to lunch mainly to tell me one thing: that I owed my professors and my college nothing; that I should decide what I wanted to do purely on the basis of what seemed best for me. In my duty-addled state, such an analysis would never have occurred to me; it was liberating. I went to law school.

In the years that followed, I became Joel's ghostwriter and grant application draftsman; his children's babysitter, his wife's confidant, and his friend. He treated me as an equal, though I was never that. I first learned in his home what unbridled love for one's children looked like, the dimensions of companionship and forgiveness within families. When, despite the difference in our years, we both became divorced at around the same time, it was he who forced his friendship through the wall of hurt that I had erected around myself, and made me talk about it. He returned to Stanford to run its development office, and I visited him and his girls there often, all the while noticing — as his wife had pointed out years before but I had ignored, such was my uncritical admiration of him — that he drank a bit too much, that his moods were becoming increasingly volatile, that his highs, which formerly seemed only the by-product of a fierce intelligence and subversive wit, were becoming disconcertingly high, his lows blackening into what only could be called severe depression.

He finally crashed completely in full public view as a senior officer of a great university, reduced in a matter of weeks from architect of a billion dollar capital campaign to a figure curled in a fetal position in bed, unable to move. (I was there for part of this disintegration, but he himself has written of it in far greater and more eloquent detail (see the archives of the Stanford alumni magazine), so I'm revealing nothing and can add little.)

I was, at first, simply, stupidly, angry at him, for ceasing to be the friend I had known, for becoming unavailable to me, for not bringing his great intellect to bear on something so paltry as a state of mind, a mere mood. It took some years for me to fully comprehend the intractable nature of depression, its ferocious toll on the human will to live, its devastating effects on everyone in the victim's life, starting with the victim himself. I was spared most of that; I only lost a friend.

Over the following decades, through the endless cycles of recovery and relapse, the shifts in treatment regimes, the hopes raised by new drugs, the shock therapy that eroded his memory, even through an eventual, short-lived remarriage, I and many other friends tried to honor in our halting ways what the man had meant to us. There were the occasional letters from him, always hand-printed in his precise way, often oddly confrontational, but never an openness to meet, never a returned call. His first wife remarried and we lost touch; his girls disappeared into their adulthoods. I missed his last official return to Denison for the inauguration of one of his successors. As I traveled on business, I would stop to have drinks with people who knew him, friends he and I had vacationed with, people who remembered the man before the crash, women who had tried to love him since, and we would trade stories of our times with him, his enormous generosity and wit, his rejections and accusations, the scary fun of his highs, the terrifying blackness of his depressions.

With time it became clear that it was a loss as permanent and non-negotiable as death, a death that couldn't be recognized for what it was, couldn't be properly mourned, because the lost one still shared the world with the bereaved.

Now that last door has closed; now we can truly mourn. Until April 10, there was yet time. There was always the chance that we could re-establish contact, that I could see him once more, sit and talk with him, forgive him and ask him to forgive me, tell him again what he meant to me, and replace that image that I carry with me always, of Joel as a brilliant, handsome young man of 36, with a true one, of Joel as an old man, still handsome I'm sure, perhaps still brilliant, but flawed and perhaps frail, and me grown old with him. What a day that would have been.

Could I have done it? Could I have done more? Of course. So when I heard he'd died, what I felt first, before I pushed the shameful feeling away, was the same feeling I'd had those many years ago when a terrible illness took Joel Smith from us: I felt sorry for myself. Death means many things, but one thing it means is that our chances are finite, and this great chance in my life had passed. But I'll say it still:

Peace to you, Joel. Peace at last.

• • •

The above account of my relationship with Joel Smith has a particular perspective that, on reflection, seems woefully one-sided, and needs a coda. It's naturally all about my memories and experience of the man and the illness that befell him midway through his life, and that's fine as far as it goes. But it's not far enough. What's missing is a recognition of the second half of his life and, more importantly, of how *he* would want to be remembered, which would be, I'm certain, very different from how I remember him.

I can only infer the elements of this other remembrance, which is itself a problem; few things irritated Joel more, especially once he became ill, than for someone to presume to understand him and the conditions under which he lived. But as he often forgave my presumptions, I'll presume again.

First and foremost, I think he would have us remember him as a sufferer of chronic depression. I used the word "victim" earlier, but I suspect he would object to that, as it is insufficiently clinical, implying something imposed from without, rather than the disease it is, usurping from within. I don't believe there are appropriately sensitive, politically correct terms to apply here, like "depressed person," or "mood-challenged person," but if there were I'm fairly sure he would have disdained them. We are not talking here about lower-case depression, the transient melancholy that is familiar to everyone who lives in the world and thinks about it. This is chronic, clinical depression, with its own fearsome constellation of symptoms, foremost among them being the loss, to varying degrees, of the ability to appreciate living itself, of the capacity to see anything but a world drained of color and purpose. Psychiatrists call its principal symptom "anhedonia"-- the inability to feel pleasure. Note the categorical flavor of that description: not diminished capacity; inability. An artisan of words like Joel might call it malignant sadness — like cancer, except it attacks the soul. William Styron, another depressed person of literary bent, called it "darkness visible." Of this much I'm sure: we, the well, can only know it by analogy, by these pale metaphors.

Which is why many of us too readily attach a moral valence to mental illness in general, and to depression in particular. Because we think we have experienced something like it, we presume to judge those who can't seem to shake it, who are drawn in by it to a place we have never been. My most shameful reactions to Joel's depression included my early belief that the supreme competence he had exhibited for the first half of this life could surely be applied to cure himself, and my disappointment when he couldn't. I might as well have urged someone with leukemia to pull himself together and get over it.

The other important fact is that depression is often as lethal as the most malignant cancer, since one human response to living a life without light is to end it.

So I believe Joel would want to be remembered as a man who lived with a pernicious, incurable disease for over forty years, and at least survived it for that long. He would, I think, want it to be seen as a life of struggle, yes, but also a life of intermittent victories, and almost unimaginable perseverance. A life — though he would never admit this — of enormous courage.

He would want to be remembered as someone who tried to make the rest of us see depression for what it is, and wrote beautifully and movingly to that end.

Just before I learned that Joel had died, I attended a dinner for the benefit of the psychiatric unit of a great university hospital. I took the opportunity to draw aside the head of the unit, and asked him what advances had been made in the last, say, thirty years in treating clinical depression, explaining that I knew someone who had it. He looked at me frankly and said, in so many words: almost none. Mood elevating drugs are still prescribed, electroshock is still administered "because it works" at least temporarily, talking therapies, generally recognized as palliatives, are pursued. It's not too much to say that none of it is reliably effective, and the reason some of it is intermittently effective isn't really understood. There simply is no "cure." This is a shame and a failure in clinical research that desperately needs to be addressed, especially since a shockingly high percentage of our population suffers from some form of clinical depression, and it is so often fatal.

I simply was not there for Joel in the second half of his life, partly because it was too difficult, and partly because that seemed to be his wish. What haunts me most in the wake of his death is the possibility that I may have gotten that last part wrong. But I believe, still, that I only reminded him of the man he had ceased to be, the times he could never recover, and that was just too painful for him.

But there were many others who were there with him through all or parts of that long journey, people I only heard about or can only imagine: the doctors, the caretakers, his fellow depressives, companions in suffering, constant and empathetic in a way that we amateurs, we worried well, could never be. He would want to be remembered by them most of all. They could speak of him honestly, and with the kind of love that only actual understanding and acceptance can confer. The rest of us, who think first only of his halcyon days, the days of early, easy triumph, of the man in his prime — the rest of us, frankly, need not apply.

Joel apparently made it clear that he wanted no memorial service after his death, and I think I know why. Too many people like me would have shown up, saying too many things like what I said in that earlier post. That would have pained him no end, since the man most of us would have been eulogizing effectively ceased to exist thirty-plus years ago, and we didn't really know the man who took his place; we would have been mourning the wrong guy. Better to shut up about it, better to go visit someone like the man he became, difficult and reclusive and maybe hard to sit in a room with; better to be certain that someone you suspect may be depressed gets help; better to make a contribution to an appropriate research organization. But no flowers, please, no pretty speeches.

He would want us to remember the right man.

April 2014

Love, Loss, and Social Security

• • •

"THE PAST IS NEVER DEAD. It's not even past," said William Faulkner. Life has a way of looping back on itself, things you thought long finished crop up like stubborn weeds, relationships tidily — or not so tidily – shelved tumble down on your head like a box of letters inadvertently dislodged when you were just trying to retrieve your old baseball glove.

A friend or enemy from long ago inevitably comes knocking. The child you had during that brief marriage in your youth becomes the mother of children who look like your mother and, like their mom, have a hammerlock on your heart. The woman with whom you had the child, the one who broke your heart and you wanted to forget becomes, unforgettably, your fellow parent and, therefore, your lifelong partner. The past is never dead; it's not even past.

The government treats you differently depending on the details of your personal history. When you pay your taxes it wants to know if you are married, or a gambler, or a student, or have dependents, or pay alimony. Not too long ago I applied to be admitted to the bar in a new home state, which involved filling out a form that required me to provide not only proof of my admittance and past practice in New York and California, but also the recitation of every place I ever lived, every job I ever had, over forty years of adult life, most of it beyond memory, lost. It was like an extended psychotherapy session. I worried that I might make some mistake, that something in the application would be discovered to be wrong, that some indelible falsity would surface as damningly as a dead body. I had to call my ex-wife – the mother of my daughter — to help fill in the blanks. She remembers everything, every address, the nuances of how we lived, neighbors and friends and co-workers of the time, furniture, street names, which restaurants we frequented, things I never paid attention to for one moment after they ceased to be part of daily life. I never dreamed when we parted that we were so permanently joined.

More recently I reached the age when one is obliged by sheer self-interest to register for Social Security. Among the many things I learned in this process is that one should defer taking benefits as long as possible, and that a surprising number of people have a potential interest in those benefits, including spouses and children, even after you're dead. The Social Security Administration will provide a printout that shows your lifetime earnings, on which your benefits are based. It's basically an x-ray of your entire working life, reduced to numbers, year by year: all those paychecks, all those withholdings, the flush times and the lean years, the earnings waxing and eventually waning, all there, and behind the numbers the dim memory of what was happening in those years, the marriages and divorces and births and deaths, the wars and recessions, the new homes, new jobs, new loves.

My first marriage was short, but there was a second one that lasted longer, in a time when we were both working too hard and enjoying our lucky lives too little. It was childless and tumultuous and probably doomed from the first, but it lasted, as many marriages do, longer than it had any right or reason to. Just over ten years, in fact. And when it ended, I paid my new ex — call her "X" — what she demanded, which was a chunk of the hard-earned money that is diagrammed in my Social Security statement, and shut her and as much of the memory of her as I could out of my life.

But the past is never dead. It turns out that X and I are lasting partners in Social Security. You see, not only do spouses have a right to claim benefits based on their marital partners' earnings, but divorced people do too – as long as they were married for at least 10 years and a day and are not currently married. So potentially X and I each can claim spousal benefits based on the other's earnings for as long as either of us lives, without reducing the benefits we can each claim based on our own earnings. In the great wisdom of the Social Security Administration, if she claims her spousal benefit, I'll never know it, and she won't know if I claim mine (unlikely, as I'm happily remarried). And unlike all the other zero-sum games that the breakup of a marriage entails, her claiming spousal benefits won't cost me a thing.

I was sure we were done, but here's this odd echo of that decade or so spent in one another's company, indelible as a tattoo.

November 2015

Life in the Silos

• • •

A WRITER FRIEND AND I were having a conversation about writing – and about a particular book idea that she had –when it struck me that she and I almost never do what we were doing so pleasurably in that moment — talk about writing — even though it's a hugely important aspect of each of our lives, and one of the most important things we have in common.

Why should this be so? It's partly a result of the guardedness that creative people carry around, the need to stake out your own space where you can make something of your own. But it isn't limited to creatives or introverts: in my former investment banking firm, we used to refer to our areas of specialization as "silos" and would try to think of ways to break them down and allow cross-pollination of ideas. This went beyond the usual "thinking outside the box" about a particular problem; we dimly perceived that our comfort zones of expertise were confining and commercially dysfunctional and we tried to make them more porous. We were rarely successful. Life inside a silo of preoccupation, specialization, bias, or shyness can be comforting. The problem arises when we forget we're inside one.

There are actual physical silos standing just outside our little Ohio town – tall metal cylinders built to contain a lot of grain on a small footprint – and they are an apt metaphor for our psychic self-confinement: dark inside, containing something homogeneous, and escapable only by deliberate extraction.

Most of us grew up believing that technology would make individual isolation purely optional: jet travel and telecommunication would neutralize distance; the Internet would empower collaboration and democratize knowledge. And some of this has happened.

But technology has also destroyed large tracts of common experience and replaced them with highly individualized pockets of perception. Not too long ago, when there were only three broadcast television networks and the idea of running a wire to your house to watch TV seemed silly, the entire nation tuned in to watch the nightly news, moon landings, presidential inaugurations, and *Bonanza*. Now our only universally shared video experience is the Super Bowl (with *Game of Thrones* perhaps a close second).

The Internet is the primary enabler of this atomization of experience, for it offers nearly endless and nearly effortless choice, and when we are allowed to choose, rather than be randomly forced up against people and ideas different from our own, we tend, over time, to choose what comforts. We pick the news feed that reinforces our political bias, the up-channel cable show that focuses on our pet interest of the moment, the app that connects us in some clever new way to people very much like ourselves. It is possible in this way to construct, gradually and even unconsciously, out of a multitude of inputs masquerading as objective information, a hermetically-sealed bubble of self-reinforcing perception. We each build our silo and climb eagerly inside.

Of course, people have always done this – subscribed to certain magazines, ignoring others, selecting friends with viewpoints similar to our own – but the building blocks of self-confinement have proliferated with the advent of social media, blogging, podcasts, and online journalism. The mesh is much finer now, the warp and weft of our personal silos much denser.

There are still some places where it's hard to build silos, because they have randomness and diversity built into them: big cities and universities come to mind. Perhaps for this reason, these places are often disturbing and we can't wait to get out of them, but if we're willing to visit for a while, and put aside our handhelds while we're there, they can remind us that an abject inability to dictate the terms on which we encounter other people and ideas can be an energizing and even ennobling condition.

But even in New York these days you can walk down a street and not encounter a single person who isn't head-down and fixated on the small computer in their hand. And even universities are under pressure to assuage the intellectual friction that gives them life and grow silos – they call them "safe spaces" – for each and every predilection, self-perceived victim, and interest group. "Trigger warnings" must be issued in advance of any possible encounter with the world outside your silo. This flight from troubling experience is the direct result of the unfettered freedom to choose – and freedom to avoid – that the modern college student has grown up with and that now, if unchecked, will ensure the further political balkanization of our society, and our future as a race of intellectual xenophobes.

Bigotry comes in many forms beyond the crude, obvious bigotry of racism or sexism. The forces of atomization and isolation that are at work around us are not always benign instruments of endless choice or brave expressions of our individuality, but potential threats to community, and we need to actively resist them. The very word "community" has been hijacked to refer to a virtually-connected horde of subscribers to this or that social media website. Twitter feeds and talk radio purvey abstracted, impersonal speech from within silos of preconception: we preach to the converted while talking past each other. How much harder it is to persuade, in person, or to seek out and give audience to opposing points of view. Yet that is what it means to live in an actual, functioning community.

In that kind of community, you sit down over coffee or a stiff drink and have a serious discussion with someone who profoundly disagrees with you about abortion, or gay marriage, or Donald Trump, or gun control, or the prospects for the Cubs making the World Series this year. You try sincerely to understand their opinion, even as you acknowledge that you can't accept it.

In that kind of community, better still, you take a walk with someone you know who is really good at something you've never done or wish you could do better – writing or wrestling; sculpture or Sudoku – and ask them to share a bit of their expertise with you. You talk about something you know you both love but somehow never get around to acknowledging to one another. Enthusiasm is motivating; a shared enthusiasm is galvanizing. You might even ask someone to teach you something you don't know and haven't a hope of learning on your own. Short of love itself, there is nothing greater to offer or receive, and the high, shiny wall of your personal silo – and mine– will be a little lower afterwards.

May 2016

The Last Place

• • •

IF I WERE ALONE – if my cherished wife were gone, my dear friends scattered to the winds, my love and work unmoored from a place, where would I choose to be? It's a useful mental exercise. The question of where on the planet you choose put your body defines, profoundly, who you are.

My brother recently announced that after over 30 years of living in the same house in Columbus with his wife, he wants to move to Boise, Idaho. He's done with living in the same place, the only place he's ever lived as an adult, and his wife has agreed to go, and he's just undergone a harrowing year of successful cancer treatment, which perhaps has something to do with it, but the choice still struck me as remarkable. They know no one in Boise, it's as far away culturally and otherwise as they could move without leaving the country, and they're discarding a foundation of familiarity as deep as it gets in most people's lives. And I'm sure that's the point. My brother wants, at least for a time, to be in a place not because he needs to be there, or because it's where he's always been, but just because he chose it.

For most of your life, as with his, family or love or work or simple habit determines where you put your body. You live where your parents live, or where you go to school, or where your lover lives, or where you come into adulthood, or where you have a job. But after a time, maybe late in life, only rarely when you are just starting out, all that falls away, and you are left with the looming question of where, in all the world, in all your corporeal essence, you belong. If your life were an itinerary, this would be the ultimate destination; this would be the last place.

The Last Place

Because this sort of choosing of place becomes possible when attachments fall away, it's partly a question of where solitude would be tolerable, or even comfortable. There's no quick answer, as most of us have little or no experience with true, protracted aloneness. Even in those brief spans of time when I technically lived alone – for part of college and law school and, briefly, after starting to work in New York, and in those backwaters of transient solitude that followed break-ups – my life was filled with people I saw daily and knew intimately – fellow students, my professors, co-workers, mentors, friends. In the law firm where I started out, we routinely worked 12-hour days, took our meals in groups of other lawyers similarly indentured. That's not really living alone in any meaningful sense, even though I returned at night to a space where no one else lived.

Then love or marriage or parenthood or friendships or all of them, if you're lucky, absolve you from solitude for most of the rest of your life, if you're lucky. The places you live have little to do with where you might be if you were alone; the question doesn't begin to present itself. In America, solitude and placelessness are indicators of something gone drastically wrong.

Even when marriages end, or loved ones die, or children grow up and leave, there are always those few friends who will be there, and by being there will fix you to a place. Some will even fight through your claims that you really want to be alone, as when a mentor-friend of mine, dead now, insisted on seeing me after my divorce, made me sit and talk about it over drinks and a long dinner, refused to let me define myself as circumstances seemed to demand: a man alone. Not on his watch. He suggested – insisted, really – that I move from the east coast to California, where he lived. And I did.

California is our national last place, out there on the left edge of the map, forever fecund with possibility, forever retreating behind its own myth. I was fleeing the bad breakup of what could have been a good marriage, I was almost middle-aged, and had been working at a job I had lost all passion for. California, and the San Francisco peninsula, was my place of personal reinvention. But I had friends there and secured a new job there before I left New York, and knew where I was going, and to whom, and more or less what waited for me. It was full of entanglements new and old, made and avoided. It was not my last place.

Friendship drew me westward then, but sometimes solitude happens and there is no one to prevent it. I can imagine that for me that could happen if my wife, who is my tether to the world, the keeper of the skein of our friendships, were gone (and no, I can't bring myself to use the other word). Part of my healing from her absence, I imagine, would be to go away too, to leave behind our house and town and all the thousand reminders of her and of our life together, and find a place that was solely mine. It would not be a place I'd lived before, with its own tangle of memories. It would be a new place, maybe the last place.

There is a purgative aspect to this leaving things behind, a sloughing off of loss by abandoning the familiar. When time for a last place comes, I imagine, I will take all my clothes to Goodwill and keep only a few shirts and blue jeans. The suits that I wore in the years in New York and San Francisco, the poles of my working life, will be given away, the dress shirts with their spread collars, the tight leather shoes with their laces, the belts and ties. Endless clothes, forgotten years of clothes, bales of it, stuffed into black plastic bags and given away. And still my excess will seem limitless. I will box up the books in the study and take them to the town library like a man taking his dog to be put down. I will enlist some neighbor boys to help move furniture out into the back yard where Goodwill can fetch it. I'd leave perhaps just a chair or two in each room, my wife's piano, our dining table. And even those things would be too much. I'd sell the house. This would be her last gift, her true bequest: escape from the thousand things that have bound me to our place, so that I can depart for another.

What would be the qualities of that other place? It would, for one thing, hold the hope of solace. It wouldn't be a place where work would be pursued, or a hobby would come to fruition, though those things might happen there. It would be chosen for its aesthetics, not its utility.

It wouldn't, therefore, be a city. Cities are utilitarian, places of distraction and challenge, not consolation, and I did the city thing when I was young, in New York, which is the distillation of all cities. It was enough, a once-and-for-all experience. Every other city, no matter where on the globe, would seem a nagging shadow of that place and time.

A quiet place, then. Probably not a seaside, where people tend to go in crowds when temporarily leaving behind their real lives. It wouldn't be a tourist town, where you're constantly distinguishing between locals and transients. I'd want to be among people who, like me, belonged to the place.

The deep woods, maybe, or in a working mountain town, or a combination of the two. Colorado has its places like this, away from the ski resorts, along rivers and streams where nobody bothers to raft.

But when all else is forgotten, when the symbolisms of birthplace and heritage and career and prestige are put aside, what beckons is the desert, the hot dry land, with mountains in the distance. The high desert around Santa Fe comes to mind, but it too is a tourist town, and my wife and I built a home there and lived there off and on, so it too would reverberate with memory.

A few years ago a cousin and her husband pulled up decades-deep stakes in a Phoenix suburb and moved to San Miquel de Allende in central Mexico, too full of retired expats for me, but they seem to love it. I lived in Mexico as a child, and the heat of the plains around Monterrey, with Saddle Mountain rising to the west, the starry chaos of the night skies there, may account for my love of deserts hemmed by hills. My memories of the place are too spotty to be encumbering; I'm remembering photographs in family albums, not what was being photographed. Mexico, maybe. *Es posible.*

The thought experiment has no conclusion, goes back on the shelf of unresolved inquiries. With any luck it will remain hypothetical. But it's worth asking: where on the planet would you place yourself, if it were just you? Who and where are you, really?

July 2016

About the Author

FOR OVER A DECADE, LAWYER and writer Keith McWalter has authored the blog *Mortal Coil*, an online compendium of political, social, occupational, and personal narrative essays. McWalter also writes for *Spoiled Guest*, a travel-related blog. In addition to publication in various newspapers, including the *New York Times*, he also won a Writer's Digest award for his first compilation of essays, *The Plastic Bag Will Not Inflate: Letters from a Bicoastal Father*. He is licensed to practice law in California, New York, and Ohio, and he and his wife Courtney divide their time between Granville, Ohio, and Sanibel, Florida.

Made in the USA
Monee, IL
11 May 2022